CW00340996

FOREVER
ENGLAND

A HISTORY OF THE NATIONAL SIDE

THE ENGLISH ASSOCIATION FOOTBALL TEAM.
England v. Scotland, 1892.

FOREVER ENGLAND

A HISTORY OF THE NATIONAL SIDE

MARK SHAOUL & TONY WILLIAMSON

TEMPUS

frontispiece: This montage of the 1892 England side was commissioned by the FA as a memento for each team member. From the top: Toone – Holt, Holmes, Shelton, Dunn, Reynolds – Hodgetts, Goodall – Chadwick, Southworth, Bassett.

First published 2000
This edition 2004

Tempus Publishing Limited
The Mill, Brimscombe Port,
Stroud, Gloucestershire, GL5 2QG
www.tempus-publishing.com

© Mark Shaoul and Tony Williamson, 2004

The right of Mark Shaoul and Tony Williamson to be identified as
the Authors of this work has been asserted in accordance with the
Copyrights, Designs and Patents Act 1988.

All rights reserved. No part of this book may be reprinted
or reproduced or utilised in any form or by any electronic,
mechanical or other means, now known or hereafter invented,
including photocopying and recording, or in any information
storage or retrieval system, without the permission in writing
from the Publishers.

British Library Cataloguing in Publication Data.
A catalogue record for this book is available from the British Library.

ISBN 0 7524 2939 6

Typesetting and origination by Tempus Publishing Limited
Printed and bound in the United Kingdom.

CONTENTS

ACKNOWLEDGEMENTS

The authors, Mark Shaoul and Tony Williamson, would like to take this opportunity to thank a few people who have helped them in the production of this, the second edition of *Forever England*. This updated edition includes many extra photographs and the new feature of an assessment of players in each era who might appropriately be considered for entry in to the England Football Hall of Fame.

Our appreciation goes to James Howarth and Tempus Publishing, who commissioned the work and assisted us in its preparation. Thanks go also to Empics, Colorsport, Associated Sports Photography and Sporting Pictures UK, who have provided most of the photographs.

Also important has been the support of our respective wives, Melissa and Sue, who have been a source of encouragement throughout.

Bobby Moore. World Cup 1966.

Having started my career in club football with Victoria United, I little believed that I would one day play for the England. Memories of my eight years with the national team are clouded with emotions that time can play some tricks with, and so I was delighted to be asked to review *Forever England* and relive some of those moments. This well-written history brings back to life many events that have charted the progress of the England team, which is after all the missionary who has taken this great game across the world.

You realise when reading this book that eight years is a brief span in the 130-plus years of our football history, but all these events are highlighted by Shaoul and Williamson's excellent coverage of early Corinthian days right through to England's recent crucial encounter with Turkey.

Meticulously researched and beautifully illustrated, with over 250 pictures, I am delighted to recommend it to you.

RON SPRINGETT

Ron Springett. Queens Park Rangers and Sheffield Wednesday goalkeeper. 33 international caps (1959-1966). Member of the England World Cup Finals squad (1962 and 1966)

CHAPTER**ONE**
THE GENTLEMEN OF ENGLAND 1870-1919

FOREVER
ENGLAND

The England story begins in 1870 with a decision by the Football Association to arrange an 'international' football fixture – a match between an English XI and a Scottish XI. The game was played at the Kennington Oval in South London on 5 March 1870. Charles Alcock recruited the English team while A.F. Kinnaird recruited the Scots. England lined up as follows:

C.W. Alcock (Old Harrovians), E.E. Bowen (Wanderers), A. Baker (Nomads), W.C. Butler (Barnes Club), W.P. Crake (Harrow School), E. Freeth (Civil Service), E. Lubbock (Old Etonians), A. Nash (Clapham Rovers), J.C. Smith (Crusaders), A.H. Thornton (Old Harrovians), R.W. Vidal (Westminster School).

Both teams were selected, by and large, from the same group of London-based players. The match ended in a 1-1 draw, with Crawford scoring for the Scots and Baker equalizing for the English with almost the last kick of the game. Two more matches followed in the 1870/71 season, England winning the game on 19 November 1-0 while there was another 1-1 draw on 25 February 1871. During the 1871/72 season, Alcock arranged two further games at the Oval between an English XI and a team of Scots who were resident in London.

In November 1871 the English beat the Scots 2-1 and then, in February 1872, the game ended 1-0, once again in favour of the English.

In order to assist in the development of the game in Scotland, which only had ten established clubs, Alcock responded positively to an invitation from the Queens Park club to bring an England XI to Glasgow to play a team of locally-based Scottish players. The contest took a little over a month to organize from the time of the meeting of the FA on 3 October 1872, when the committee had concluded that: 'In order to further the interests of the Association in Scotland, it was decided during the current season that a team should be sent to Glasgow to represent England'.

A few weeks later, on 30 November 1872, a team of English footballers arrived at the West of Scotland Cricket Ground at Partick in Glasgow to play the Scots. It was this game that was forever to be recognized as the first official international match between two countries. Seven of the English side had the luxury of staying overnight before the game at the Royal Garrick Hotel in Glasgow, while the other four, who were unable to travel north the day before the game, took the sleeper train, arriving on the morning of the match.

above: A ticket for the first official international match in Glasgow. A crowd of 4,000 paid the 1s entrance fee.

left: Charles Alcock, a founding father of the game and the driving force behind the first official international match versus Scotland in 1872. He planned to play in that game but, due to injury, finished up officiating as one of the umpires.

The England team, selected by Alcock, was drawn from nine clubs. The team included representatives of both Oxford and Cambridge Universities, the Army, the Wanderers, and just two clubs that survive in the professional game today: Notts County and The Wednesday (who were to change their name to Sheffield Wednesday in 1929). Crystal Palace was also represented, but this was not the club we know today. What is interesting to note is that we see here an England team selected from a nationwide spread of teams. The FA's influence at this time suffered from a North/South divide and one of the reasons for actively including players from the Midlands and North was to curry favour with their sides and attract them to play in the FA Cup. England's line-up for the game in Glasgow comprised of a goalkeeper, one back, one half-back and eight forwards, as follows:

W.J. Maynard (1st Surrey Rifles),
E.H. Greenhalgh (Notts County), R. de Welch (Wanderers), F.B. Maddison (Oxford University), R. Barker (Hertfordshire Rangers),
J. Brockbank (Cambridge University),
J.C. Clegg (The Wednesday), A.K. Smith (Oxford University), C.J. Ottaway (Oxford University), C.J. Chenery (Crystal Palace),
C.J. Morice (Barnes).

Alcock, a prolific striker with the Wanderers, had justifiably included himself in the original England eleven, but an injury prevented him from playing in and captaining the first official England team. He had to be content with running the line as one of the referee's two umpires, the other being a local, H. Smith. The honour of captaining England went to the side's best forward, Cuthbert Ottaway. Just twenty-two years old at the time,

Ottaway was the youngest player to lead out an England side until Bobby Moore in 1963.

The England team wore white jerseys (sporting a crest of three lions), white knickerbockers and dark blue caps. The Scots provided the referee, William Keay.

Alcock, along with most commentators, was confident of an England victory, and his side dominated most of the game. However, he had underestimated the Scots, particularly in their defensive abilities. The England attack was kept at bay, while the advantage of having all eleven players coming from one club was clearly helping the Scots against an England team that had never even trained together before the day of the match. The home side was every bit the England team's equal and were reported to have come closest to winning. However, despite playing in front of a satisfyingly large crowd of 4,000, the match ended in a goalless draw – a scoreline that was not to be repeated for ninety-eight years of games between these two oldest rivals in world football.

Probably more important than the result was the fact that the event, which financially and logistically had been a risky endeavour, had been a success and had raised £102 – a significant sum in 1872.

England's selection process for the Glasgow game had been very straightforward: Alcock had simply selected the team himself to join him for the trip to Glasgow. However, for the return match in London in March 1873, he arranged a series of trial matches to which leading clubs were invited to send players. This process resulted in only two players from the first England XI surviving to play in the second game: Ernest

Greenhalgh and Chenery. Alcock, recognizing the merit of the Scots' formation, adopted a similar approach to his rivals and the changes brought success.

The team of 1873, a notably stronger one than the previous year, beat the Scots in front of a 3,000 crowd at the Oval. England's superior dribbling skills saw them take an early 2-0 lead. The Scots fought back to level the scores at 2-2, but England had the final say, scoring twice more to win 4-2. Two players from the FA Cup-winning side of that year, the Wanderers, scored for England. Alex Bonsor scored England's opening goal while William Kenyon-Slaney, a captain in the Household Cavalry, added two more. Captain Chenery also got on the scoresheet, while the luckless Alcock again missed the game through injury. The FA recorded a profit of over £70 from the game and the cash was at once earmarked for the trip to Glasgow the following year. So it was that the series of annual fixtures, alternating between London and Glasgow, began to take shape.

However, England's successes in the early years of competition with the Scots were few and far between. The victory in 1873 was to be repeated just twice over the following nineteen years as the Scots dominated the encounters between the two countries. It was not that the English could not field a strong or skilful eleven, but the Scots' power came from picking their side around one team, Queens Park.

England's first defeat came in March 1874 in the third official game. The Scots team, which included seven from Queens Park, gained a worthy 2-1 win in front of 7,000 spectators. On the final whistle Harry McNeil, the midfield star

1878 and the game is in progress: England attack the Scottish goal – presumably hoping not to hit the crossbar.

of the side, was carried shoulder-high from the field as the celebrations in Glasgow began.

Alcock finally won his one and only England cap in 1875. Awarding himself the captaincy, the Association's Secretary and sometime Wanderers forward was reported to have been very pleased when he scored for England in the game. His only disappointment must have been that his goal was not a winning one for his team since the game ended in a 2-2 draw.

This drawn match was followed by three consecutive Scottish victories. The first, 3-0 north of the border, was followed by a 3-1 scoreline in London. This was an excellent result for the Scots, only to be bettered the following year in the famous 7-2 demolition of England at the Old Hampden ground in Glasgow in 1879 – the only time a full England team has conceded as many as seven goals against another British side. Following that humiliation, and three years after Scotland had begun playing against Wales, Alcock arranged a second England fixture for the 1878/79 season, also against the Principality. England won 2-1 at the Oval in front of a sparse crowd of 200 – officially the lowest turnout ever to witness a full England game.

The win was followed later in the season, in April 1879, by a rare victory over the Scots, which saw England victorious by the odd goal in nine. Amazingly, England were 4-1 down at half time and facing a defeat of the same magnitude as the previous year. But this time England were not o be beaten. Their saviour was Charlie Bambridge, a twenty-year old playing in his debut match. The Swifts' winger was known as a skilful footballer with great pace and he lived up to his reputation in the second half, scoring a solo goal after picking up the ball on the halfway line. Then, in the final minutes of the game, he scored again, this time the winning goal for England: these were his first two of 11 goals in 18 games for his country, Bambridge becoming the first player to reach double figures in goals scored for England.

While both sets of fans showed great support for their club league and cup competitions, the highlight of the season for all Scots was the international fixture against the English. In March 1880, a new record attendance was set when 20,000 turned up for the game, the first to be played at the new Hampden Park. The crowd was kept fully entertained as nine goals were scored

N.L. Jackson, the FA Assistant Secretary, started the Corinthians club in the 1880s, in an effort to drive up the standards of the English player. As a result of his action, the national team's performances improved.

harlie Bambridge, England's first star striker, who scored two goals n a match-winning debut in 1879.

for the third year running. They were also pleased by the result, since the Scots won 5-4.

The 1880/81 season that followed was a particularly bad one for England. Not only did they lose 6-1 at the Oval to the Scots, but the team also lost to Wales for the first time, going down 1-0 at the home of Blackburn Rovers.

During the 1881/82 season, England added a third fixture, crossing the Irish Sea to Belfast to play Ireland for the first time. The Irish performance was very poor and no match for a less-than-full-strength England. The visitors ran out winners by a record margin, 13-0. Two England forwards scored hat-tricks for the first time: Oliver Vaughton (who scored the first hat-trick and went on to bag five goals in the game) and Arthur Brown (who scored four in total). Both players were making their international debuts; it was also a proud moment for Aston Villa since both were from the Midlands club.

The result was small consolation for the FA and England's supporters when later in the season, in March 1882, England lost first to the Scots in Glasgow by five goals to one and then days later to the Welsh in Wrexham by five goals to three. These were dark days for the England side.

The next major development in the history of the game was the introduction of the first program of games to be viewed as a 'league': the Home Championship. The results of the six matches between England, Scotland, Wales and Ireland were now aggregated to identify a British Isles champion. The Home Championship was to continue, only interrupted by two world wars, until 1984 – by which time this domestic tournament was deemed obsolete by the combined weight of competitive World Cup and European Championship fixtures.

In that inaugural year, the Scots, still alone in successfully employing a passing game, won all three of their matches, scoring ten goals and conceding just one, against Wales. The game against England was a close-run affair but the Scots won 1-0 to take the title.

1883/84 HOME CHAMPIONSHIP FINAL TABLE

	P	W	D	L	GF	GA	P
Scotland	3	3	0	0	10	1	6
England	3	2	0	1	12	2	4
Wales	3	1	0	2	7	8	2
Ireland	3	0	0	3	1	19	0

In the twelve years from the first official international against Scotland in 1872 up to and including this first Home Championship in the 1883/84 season, England had played 22 games. They had won all three against Ireland, had won four out of six against Wales but had only managed to beat Scotland twice in thirteen attempts.

However, the fabric of English football was changing rapidly. Inside the Association, Alcock had been perceptive enough to realize that professionalism represented the future of the game and was not slow in introducing waged footballers into the England side. It would not be long before the gentlemen players of the capital city would be replaced by the professionals from clubs in the booming industrial towns of the Midlands and the North. But while the English grasped the nettle of professionalism and began selecting players from the likes of Preston North End, Blackburn Rovers, Nottingham Forest and West Bromwich Albion, the Scots remained

Norman Bailey was awarded 19 caps between 1878 and 1887 and won an FA Cup winners' medal with Clapham Rovers in 1879. Apart from his commitment to the FA, he was a practising solicitor.

stubbornly faithful to the amateur code, a decision that would cost them dearly in the years to come.

James Forrest, the Blackburn Rovers centre half, became the first officially recognized professional England international when he was selected for the 1885 team for the Home Championship games and paid a wage of ten shillings. Forrest's international career spanned 11 appearances while, in club football, he won a record 5 FA Cup winners' medals.

The 1884/85 season saw England beat Ireland 4-0 in Manchester then draw with Wales in Blackburn. An unlikely win over the Scots would

have secured the Home Championship title, but the teams drew 1-1 and the honours went to Scotland. The following season, 1885/86, England took a share of the spoils. Ireland and Wales had proved easy meat for England and a 1-1 draw for the second year running against the Scots gave them five points. Although Scotland also beat the Welsh and Irish, with goal difference not counting in the Scots' favour, the title was shared. The hero of the series for England was new cap Tinsley Lindley, who scored in all three games. Lindley played for Nottingham Forest and Cambridge University but he soon found his way into the famed Corinthians set-up. In all, Lindley played 13 times for England, captaining his country on at least 4 occasions, and scoring 14 goals to follow Bambridge into the England goal-scoring charts.

After another second place in the Home Championship behind the Scots in 1886/87, England finally triumphed in the 1887/88 season. The campaign had begun with the introduction of the FA's new International Selection Committee and finished with outright victory in the Home Championship for the first time. The old selection procedure had got out of hand as upwards of 70 players would turn up for the trials, making the process a logistical and bureaucratic nightmare for Alcock and his team. In its place came the Selection Committee. Comprising seven men, the committee announced a team on the basis of who had won the most votes at the end of more limited trials.

The 1888 victory against the Scots was long overdue and, remarkably, England's first north of the border. Their goals came from Lindley, Dennis Hodgetts, Fred Dewhurst (2) and John Goodall. Although both of Goodall's parents were Scottish,

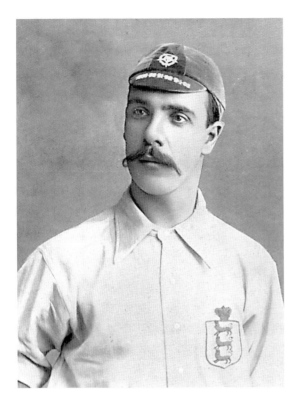

above: P.M. & A.M Walters: a pair of traditional Corinthian full-backs who played for England between 1885 and 1890.

left:: John Goodall, who scored two goals in a match-winning debut in 1879.

and while his brother played for Ireland, a record of 11 goals in 14 appearances for England clearly demonstrated the allegiance of probably the best ball-player of the era.

The formation of the new Football League helped to continue the improvement witnessed in the standards of English football and in England's domination of the international scene: between 1888 and 1896 England would lose just once in 26 games.

The first five games between England and Scotland played in England had all been staged in London at the Oval. Then, in 1883, the FA chose to play the Scots outside London, in Sheffield. They followed that with two more Scotland games away from the capital, in 1887 and 1891, when both were played in Blackburn. However, for the 1891 game, the selectors overlooked the players from the Rovers and Olympic teams and the townsfolk, showing their loyalty to club in preference to country, promptly refused to turn up to the game in the numbers expected, a game that England won 2-1. To add insult to indignation, the town also fell victim that year to the very first invasion by Scots fans as 500 descended on the Lancashire town for the game.

While England were now achieving longed-for success in the Home Championship, Alcock again looked to the Association's wider role in developing the game of football and arranged a first international match against non-British opponents, a visiting Canadian side. The game, which was played at the Oval on 19 December 1891, was viewed at the time as a full international but has never been accredited as such, since the Canadian side was not selected by a recognized national association. However, strictly speaking, neither had the first official game against the Scots but the validity of that match is never questioned. For the record, England beat the Canadians 6-1.

England's dominance was throwing up a number of stars. One player of much renown from this time was the diminutive Billy Bassett. Bassett, of West Bromwich Albion, prowled the wing to good effect in 16 England matches between 1888 and 1896. During this spell in the England side, he scored 8 goals and assisted in many more, most notably in 1893 when, in ten minutes, he laid on three goals for team-mates to turn around a match which England looked like losing to the Scots.

Another star in the England team was Gilbert Oswald Smith, an amateur with the Old Carthusians and Oxford University. He did not have the speed of some other players, but was famed for his

One of the earliest known England team photographs: the side that played Wales in 1891. From left to right, back row: Brann (Swifts), Porteous (Sunderland), Wilkinson (Old Carthusians), Jackson (Oxford University), Clegg (Umpire). Middle row: Smith (Nottingham Forest), Holt (Everton), Shelton (Notts County), Millward (Everton). Front row: Goodall (Derby County), Southworth (Blackburn Rovers), Chadwick (Everton).

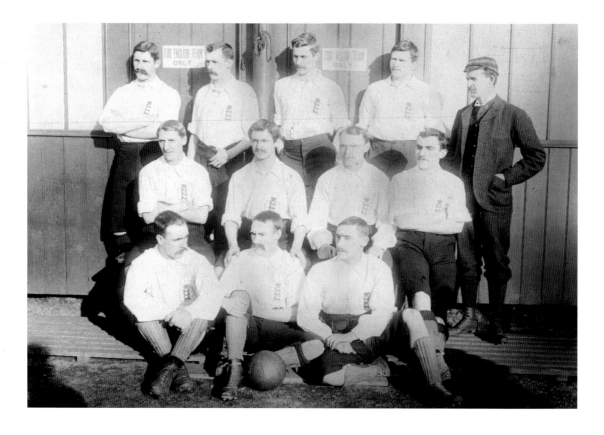

above: The England team that defeated Scotland 5-2 at Richmond in April 1893. From left to right, back row: McGregor (FA), Gosling, Bentley (FA), Holt (FA), Clegg (FA), Kinsey (FA), Holmes (FA), Goodall (FA). Middle row: Bassett (FA), Reynolds (FA), Cotterill (FA), Gay (FA), Harrison (FA). Front row: Spiksley (FA), Chadwick (FA).

left: Billy Bassett accumulated 16 caps and 8 goals for England between 1886 and 1896. He was a great winger, both for his country and for his club, West Bromwich Albion, whom he served as player, director and chairman.

ability both to run with the ball and to shoot with the instep, as opposed to only with the toe. He played 20 times for England between 1893 and 1901, captaining the side in more than half of these appearances and accruing 11 goals for his country in the process.

Of even greater fame was Steve Bloomer. In 1896, in just his second season in England's colours, Bloomer netted five goals in the 9-1 demolition of Wales. Although there is some disagreement over the Derby County centre forward's tally that day,

what is not in doubt is that Bloomer was a goal machine. Probably England's most famed player from the pre-First World War era, Bloomer was capped 23 times over twelve years and scored 28 goals for England. Unsurprisingly, Bloomer set many records, including the outstanding achievement of scoring in all of his first ten matches for England – a record that remains unbeaten.

In November 1899, with the century drawing to a close, the Association took another great step forward, sponsoring a four-match unofficial

England tour of Germany. As ever, the Association's prime motivation was to support the growth of the game, this time outside Britain. The tour was a success on and off the field when the side easily beat the Germans three times and also defeated a combined German-Austrian side in the fourth game. Two years later, the Germans sent a side to England for two games. Both were won by the Association's England teams: an amateur side beat the visitors 12-0 while England's professional team beat the Germans 10-0. All these matches have been considered unofficial – according to the history books England's first official match with Germany would be in 1930.

Back home, England continued to dominate the Home Championship. From 1900 until the outbreak of the First World War, England won outright or took a share in ten of fourteen titles. The 1902 game between England and Scotland at Ibrox Park, Glasgow, was overshadowed by disaster. In British football's first tragedy, twenty-five people were killed and many more injured after part of the terracing collapsed. Many spectators at the game were not even aware of the

A pre-match team group photograph of players selected for the England v. Scotland game at Goodison in April 1895. From left to right, back row: Jackson, Lodge, Reynolds, Reid (referee), Holt, Sutcliffe, Needham, Crabtree, Lythgoe, Hughes. Front row: Bassett, Bloomer, Goodall, Gosling, S. Smith.

Football's first major crowd disaster occurrs at the match versus Scotland at Ibrox in April 1902. Makeshift stretchers are used to carry away the dead and injured.

disaster since the match continued. However, the full extent of the tragedy became apparent after the game had finished and later the result was declared void. The match was replayed the following month at Villa Park. The replayed game ended in a 2-2 draw, with all proceeds going to the disaster fund.

By 1905, the team selection process had an established format that built up through the season. The international season would begin with a trial involving teams of amateur and professional players based in the South. These players were then whittled down in number to an XI who would play a team of professionals from the Midlands and North. This trial assisted the Committee in selecting a team for the first international of the year, against Ireland. This game then served as a trial for the tougher Welsh game, which, in turn, helped to fine-tune the team to face the Scots.

Looking outside the regular fixtures against the home countries, England had now played a handful of unofficial games, but it was not until the summer of 1908 that the national side played its first official games against non-British sides. An ambitious tour of Central Europe took in a crowded schedule of four games in one week in June. The first game of the tour was in Vienna against Austria. The England team for this historic encounter lined up as follows:

Bailey (Leicester Fosse), Crompton (Blackburn Rovers), Corbett (Birmingham), Warren (Derby County), Wedlock (Bristol City), Hawkes (Luton Town), Rutherford (Newcastle United), Woodward (Tottenham Hotspur), Hilsdon (Chelsea), Windridge (Chelsea), Bridgett (Sunderland).

The team-sheet page taken from a rare programme from the England v. Scotland encounter in Sheffield in 1903.

Captained by Vivian Woodward, England won this first game 6-1 then, two days later, crushed the Austrians 11-1 before putting seven past Hungary. England then played Bohemia (not a country in its own right but a province of the Austro-Hungarian Empire). England's opposition was drawn from the Prague-based Slavia club, who were managed at that time by a Scotsman. England won the game 4-0, relying on a dubious penalty decision from the English referee when the score was only 1-0 to calm the nerves and set up the victory. The win closed a successful, if rather one-sided, tour. The FA and the squad returned home, having confirmed in their own minds England's status as the best in Europe.

England's only other matches against Continental opposition before the First World War came on a second tour the next year, in 1909, following a satisfactory clean sweep in the Home Championship. On the tour England won all three games, beating Austria once and Hungary twice. Robert Crompton, the Blackburn Rovers right-back, wrote his own chapter in the history of England when, in March 1911, he stepped out against Wales for his 24th England cap, thereby beating Bloomer's record. The match, played at Millwall's ground in South London, ended in a comfortable 3-0 win for England. Crompton was one of the leading lights

The team, minus Vivian Woodward, relax prior to the 1905 game against Scotland. From left to right, back row: Ruddlesdin, Bridgett, H. Smith, Sharp, Roberts, Linacre. Front row: Spencer, Bache, Bloomer, Leake.

Lyall, Scotland's goalkeeper, gathers the ball as Bloomer closes in and Thomson appeals, 1905.

England v Wales, 1905. From left to right (team only), standing: Bond, Linacre, Roberts, Leake, Woodward, Smith, Hardman. Seated: Harris, Bloomer, Spencer, Wolstenholme.

left: Woodward was a regular selection for England over a period spanning 1903 to 1911 and gained 23 caps, scoring 29 goals. Including all amateur appearances, he totalled 67 caps, claiming 86 goals. He also won two Olympic gold medals with the Great Britain sides of 1908 and 1912.

right: Bob Crompton joins Billy Meredith of Manchester United for the toss before the game against Wales in March 1912.

of English football in the pre-war days. Capped 41 times over an incredible 12 seasons, he held many England records for a number of years, while his total number of caps would have been even higher but for the selectors' insistence on having an amateur England captain for the overseas tours of 1908 and 1909.

England won the 1910/11 Home Championship outright, shared the title with Scotland in 1911/12, and then won it outright again in 1912/13. However, the 1913/14 campaign was to be a season that England would want to forget. They began with a 3-0 reverse at Middlesbrough, the first time England had lost to the Irish on English soil. Two days later, England beat Wales 2-0 in Cardiff. Scotland had drawn against both Ireland and Wales, so the Glasgow match would decide

which of the teams would finish the season as runners-up to the Irish.

The result went the Scots' way, 3-1, and England, for whom Fleming scored, finished third in the Home Championship. The game was also to be the last international match played before war broke out.

The 1914/15 season was set against the backdrop of the First World War. The British associations came to a joint decision against proceeding with the Home Championship, although England's two controlling bodies, the Football League and the FA, decided that both of their club competitions would continue as planned.

Of the eleven Englishmen who competed against the Scots back in the spring of 1914, five would represent their country again when international

E.H. LINTOTT.

Evelyn Lintott, of Queens Park Rangers and Bradford City, won 7 caps. He was killed while on active service on the Somme.

To-Day's Teams

England v. Ireland.

Ayresome Park, Saturday, February 14, 1914.
Referee: Mr A. A. Jackson (Scotland).
Kick-off at 3 o'clock.

ENGLAND.

RIGHT   LEFT

Hardy
(Aston Villa).

Crompton,   Pennington.
(Blackburn Rovers).   (West Bromwich Albion).

Cuggy,   Buckley,   Watson.
(Sunderland).   (Derby County).   (Burnley).

Wallace,   Shea,   Elliott,   Latheron,   Martin.
(Aston Villa).   (Blackburn).   (Middlesbrough).   (Blackburn).   (Sunderland).

Thompson,   McAuley,   Gillespie,   Young,   Lacey.
(Clyde).   (Preston N.E.).   (Sheffield United).   (Linfield).   (Liverpool).

Hamill,   O'Connell,   Hampton.
(Manchester United).   (Hull City).   (Bradford City).

Craig,   W. G. McConnell.
(Greenock Morton).   (Bohemians).

F. W. McKee.
(Belfast Celtic).

LEFT   RIGHT

IRELAND.

The team-sheet from the 1914 match against Ireland, which the Irish won 3-0 – their first victory on English soil.

football resumed in the spring of 1919. During the course of the war many professionals signed up and died in action, including some who had pulled on the England shirt. One was the amateur Evelyn Lintott, the Queens Park Rangers and Bradford City left-half, who was also one of the first chairmen of the Players' Union. Lintott, who won 7 caps, died on the Somme. Steve Bloomer had gone to Berlin in July 1914 to coach. As the conflict escalated, he (along with two other English professionals) was interned for the duration of the war.

BOB CROMPTON
Blackburn Rovers
Right-back
41 international caps (1902-1914)

Bob Crompton has a record that most other international players can only dream of. Playing for the premier club of his era, he was an automatic choice for the national team for 13 years. Capped 41 times, he captained England in 23 of those matches. His appearances record lasted until 1952 when Billy Wright made his 42nd appearance for England. It is unlikely that anyone will hold an England record for as long again.

STEVE BLOOMER
Derby County/Middlesbrough
Inside right
23 international caps (1895-1907)

The first truly great goalscorer – who at one time was both the player with the most caps for his country and the top marksman. His 26 goals were accumulated over thirteen years of playing for England and he scored in both the first and the final game. His tally remained the record for some fifty years until it was surpassed by Nat Lofthouse in 1956. It was in 1895 that he made his first appearance, versus Scotland – something he would do for ten successive years: yet another record.

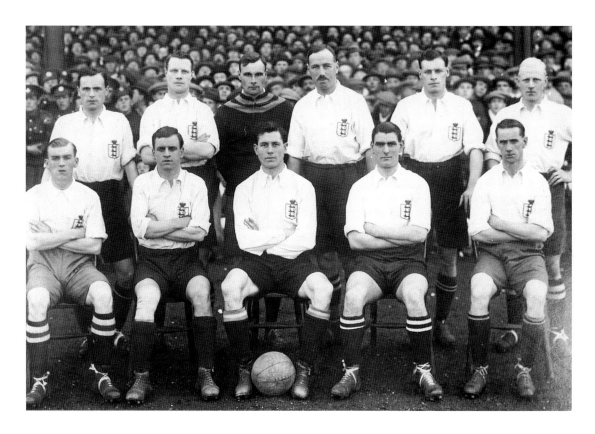

Ireland against England at Belfast, 25 October 1919. England's team in the 1-1 draw was, from left to right, back row: Bagshaw, J. Smith, Hardy, Knight, Bowser, Watson. Front row: Turnbull, Carr, Cock, Joe Smith, Hodgkinson.

International football returned in the spring of 1919 with two 'Victory' matches against Scotland and then two against Wales. The Home Championship resumed in the autumn of 1919, midway through the first League season after the war. For their first game, England took a side to Belfast to play the Irish with just two players who had played for England before the war: the incomparable goalkeeper Sam Hardy and inside left Joe Smith.

However, the Irish proved to be no pushovers and held their more illustrious opponents to a 1-1 draw. Worse was to follow for England against the Welsh at Highbury when they were defeated, by two goals to one. The series ended for England with a cracking match against Scotland at Sheffield, a game that England had to win to avoid taking the wooden spoon. The *Daily Mail* reporter, Alfred Davis, called it 'one of the best internationals seen for many a long day – full of dramatic incident right up to the last kick'. He was not wrong. Inspirational goalkeeping from Campbell in the Scots' goal and an outstanding display of sharp-shooting from his forwards saw the Scots reach a 4-2 lead by half-time. Despite this setback, England were not in the mood to capitulate and,

In October 1919 a Victory international was played between the Football Associations of Wales and England at Cardiff: England's Knight and Wales' Meredith start the proceedings.

Sam Hardy, of Liverpool and Aston Villa, won 21 international caps over the period 1907 to 1920. He was generally recognized to be the best English goalkeeper in the first fifty years of international competition.

at the break, felt they had performed better than the scoreline showed. The white shirts poured forward in the second half and sure enough, after 67 minutes, the Scots' defence was breached when Burnley's Bob Kelly halved the deficit. His striking partner, West Bromwich Albion's Fred Morris, levelled the scores within 60 seconds and just five minutes later Kelly netted his second to put England into a 5-4 lead from which the Scots did not recover.

The 1919/20 season ended with that nine-goal thriller against Scotland but it proved to be a rather inauspicious farewell to one of England's all-time greats, Hardy. In a thirteen-year career that had seen him play for England 21 times he had set new standards in goalkeeping and had become a role model for a generation of 'keepers. It was not often that he conceded four for club or country and this last match had been something of a freak occurrence.

Following the war, England and the other British sides had refused to play against their wartime foes: Germany, Austria and Hungary. Then, in December 1919, England extended this self-imposed ban to include any other countries that had subsequently played against these three. Since this now included a number of other European nations, the position of the British associations within FIFA quickly became untenable and they formally withdrew on 23 April 1920.

ENGLAND

England's European isolation lasted one year. In March 1921 they played Belgium, who had not played any of the three Central Powers. The game was played in Brussels and England won 2-0 with goals from Charlie Buchan of Sunderland and Henry Chambers of Liverpool. Also in the side was Jack Fort of Millwall who, in winning his first and only England cap, became the first player to be picked for England while playing for a Third Division side.

Two years later the Belgians became the very first overseas side to play an official international in England when they stepped out at Highbury in March 1923. Belgium proved to be no match for

The England team that played in the first international game to be held at the Hawthorns, 1922. From left to right, back row: Osbourne, Moss, Taylor, Grimsdell, Harrow. Front row: Mercer, Smith, Seed, Wilson, Chambers, Williams.

HEADQUARTERS—

EUSTON HOTEL, LONDON.

Players, Reserves and Members of the Selection Committee will please make their own travelling arrangements.

All Players unable to travel on Monday morning, March 19th, and report at Headquarters by 11.30 a.m., must travel on Sunday. Rooms will be reserved for Players at the Euston Hotel, but it is important Players requiring accommodation should notify me per return post.

Players able to travel on Monday morning must report at the Euston Hotel not later than 11.30 a.m.

Shirts and knickers will be provided by the Football Association.

Luncheon for Players will be served at 12.30 sharp. Luncheon for Committee and Guests at 1 p.m.

In the event of a player being unable to play he must telegraph immediately to "Football Association, Westcent, London."

The Teams will be entertained to Dinner at the Holborn Restaurant after the match at 6.30 p.m.

The receipt of this itinerary **must** be acknowledged by players immediately to—

G. WAGSTAFFE SIMMONS,
Member of Selection Committee in Charge.

29, Chambers Lane,
N.W. 10.
Tele : Central 173.

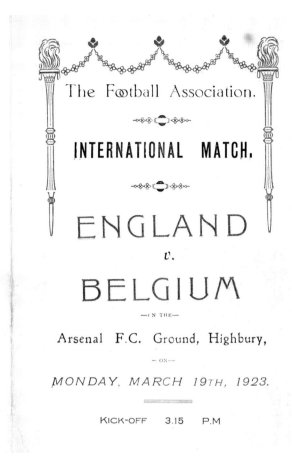

The Football Association.

INTERNATIONAL MATCH.

ENGLAND

v.

BELGIUM

—ON THE—

Arsenal F.C. Ground, Highbury,

— ON —

MONDAY, MARCH 19TH, 1923.

KICK-OFF   3.15   P.M

A rare international itinerary for England *v.* Belgium, Highbury, March 1923.

the English, who rattled up six goals to which the Belgians replied just once. These two victories were much needed in the post-war years. In four seasons of Home Championships, England had mustered just four wins, two against the Irish and one each against the Welsh and Scots. These easy victories against Belgium provided a welcome distraction and gave the English a taste for European opposition. In May 1923, England continued to gain experience against Continental opposition with one game against France in Paris, which they

won 4-1, and two against Sweden in Stockholm, both of which were won: 4-2 and 3-1.

However, at home England's poor form continued. The 1923/24 campaign began with a 2-1 defeat by the Irish in Belfast. Days later, the England side, including just two players from the Irish defeat, went to Brussels for England's third game against the Belgians. The resulting 2-2 draw was a disappointment and broke England's one hundred percent record against Continental teams. This was followed by a 2-1 defeat at the hands of the Welsh. Now, in the spring of 1924, England's disappointing season was to end with their first game in the shadows of the Twin Towers as they entertained the Scots at Wembley for the first time. England lined up as follows:

> Taylor (Huddersfield Town), Smart (Aston Villa), Wadsworth (Huddersfield Town), Moss (Aston Villa), Spencer (Newcastle United), Barton (Birmingham), Butler (Bolton Wanderers), Jack (Bolton Wanderers), Buchan (Sunderland), Walker (Aston Villa), Tunstall (Sheffield United).

No one could have foreseen that England would have lost their games against Wales and Ireland and that now the white shirts would be facing a whitewash. England had never finished bottom of the Home Championship and had to beat the Scots, who had two points to England's nought, just to take a share of the wooden spoon. The selectors brought back Charlie Buchan – without doubt the best centre forward at their disposal. His influence was at once apparent but he could not carry the side alone and the game ended in a 1-1 draw. The result consigned England to the wooden spoon and also began the team's long association with Wembley in the most inauspicious of ways.

The following year, 1924/25, England beat Wales and Ireland only to lose to the Scots in the title decider at Hampden Park. The season after that, 1925/26, England again finished bottom of the heap.

Scotland's obsession with beating England was even noted by The Times' football correspondent in 1925, who reported that the Scots in the crowd that day refused to accept the possibility of defeat whereas the less vociferous English seemed to be

Scotland came to Wembley Stadium in April 1924 to play the first international football match at the 'Twin Towers'. A great occasion, this first encounter resulted in a 1-1 draw.

almost indifferent as to the result. From 1872 to 1927, England won only 16 times to Scotland's 22, a remarkable achievement for Scotland considering the numbers of players available for both sides to select from.

Scotland's second visit to Wembley was in March 1928. They had little to fear since England had already lost to Ireland and Wales but, unlike in previous years, they uncharacteristically gambled on the result by bringing a largely untried side to the capital.

The Scots team, henceforth dubbed the 'Wembley Wizards', were in irresistible form that day and their 5-1 win has been widely recognized

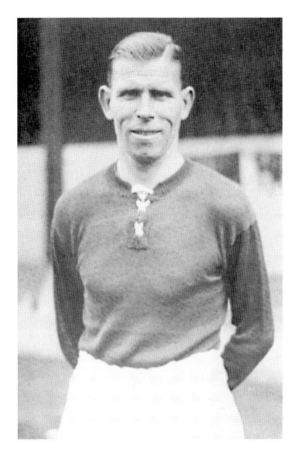

above: A 2-1 win at Swansea gave this England side a fine start to the Home Championship. From left to right. back row: Kelly, Cook, Roberts, Pym, Spencer, Dorrell. Front row: Ashurst, Walker, Bower, Hill, Graham.

left: Charlie Buchan, the London boy who made good in the North East with Sunderland. Originally capped in 1913, he had a surprise recall to the English team for the first Wembley international. He won 6 caps in total, spread over eleven years. He later became a leading sports journalist.

as the most emphatic victory over England in the history of games between the two countries. The defeat of England gave the Scots their first victory in London since 1897 and consigned England to the wooden spoon in the Home Championship.

Leaving the Scots to celebrate a famous win, England went first to Paris and then to Antwerp on a two-match tour. Both games ended in triumph for England. The first saw England notch up five goals, with Everton's Dixie Dean helping himself to a brace, and the Derby County number ten George Stephenson doing likewise. Dean added two more to his tally in the 3-1 win over Belgium, boosting his international total to 16 in 10 games.

Dean was to score just twice more in his remaining six games for England. Although he had been prolific for Everton, his England scoring record against the home countries was not impressive, standing at 5 goals in 10 games – compared with 13 goals in 6 games against Continental sides.

In the 1927/28 Home Championship, England lost all three games for the first time. The next year, following victories over Wales and Ireland, England's fortunes changed and, once more, they were presented with the possibility of winning the tournament. However, this success was denied them as the Scots won 1-0 at Hampden Park to take the title outright for the sixth time in nine years.

The England team for the home game against Scotland in March 1928. The Scots came to Wembley on a losing run and returned home with a resounding 5-1 win – and a place in history as they earned the title of 'Wembley Wizards'.

altogether than France and Belgium and won the game in Madrid 4-3.

England's fortunes turned the corner in the 1929/30 season. Convincing wins over Ireland and Wales had seen England score nine goals without conceding any in return. Scotland too had beaten Ireland and Wales. The showdown for the Home Championship title would not only determine the supremacy of one over the other but, if England were to win, might just signify a new start for England. The England side for this crucial game, which included four players from the runaway winners of the First Division, Sheffield Wednesday, lined up as follows:

Hibbs (Birmingham), Goodall (Huddersfield Town), Blenkinsop (Sheffield Wednesday), Strange (Sheffield Wednesday), Webster (Middlesbrough), Marsden (Sheffield Wednesday), Crooks (Derby City), Jack (Arsenal), Watson (West Ham United), Bradford (Birmingham), Rimmer (Sheffield Wednesday).

After the season ended, England went on a three-match European tour. France and Belgium were now regular opponents and, with a confidence not displayed at home, England made light work of both, this time winning 4-1 and 5-1 respectively. The Middlesbrough centre forward George Camsell scored six of these goals. At twenty-six years old, Camsell had come late to the England team, but swiftly made up for any lost time with a very impressive return, finishing his international career with a stunning tally of 18 goals in just 9 games over seven years. The third game of the tour was against a new opponent, Spain. The Spanish were a tougher proposition

The game went England's way. A strike from David Jack and two each from Vic Watson and Ellis Rimmer gave England five goals, to which the Scots replied just twice. England had won the Home Championship for the first time since 1913.

Dixie Dean – the archetypal bustling centre forward. Good in the air and when controlling the ball, he scored 18 goals in his 16 appearances for England. His tally of 60 goals in a season for Everton in 1927/28 remains a record for the top flight of English football.

1929/30 HOME CHAMPIONSHIP FINAL TABLE

	P	W	D	L	GF	GA	P
England	3	3	0	0	14	2	6
Scotland	3	2	0	1	9	8	4
N. Ireland	3	1	0	2	8	6	2
Wales	3	0	0	3	2	17	0

England were now regular visitors to the Continent – friendly internationals had become an established feature of the international football scene – but they were to play no part in the next major development for the game. After years of planning, FIFA took the initiative and arranged the first World Cup tournament for the summer of 1930. Uruguay was an appropriate choice of venue since the South Americans were the Olympic champions. FIFA were keen to have the British participate in the inaugural tournament, but their overtures fell on deaf ears.

A humorous view of England's 5-2 victory over Scotland in 1930.

Undeterred by a number of rebuttals, FIFA carried on regardless. The competition, comprising thirteen teams, was won by the home nation, who beat Argentina 4-2 in the final. England's summer games for 1930 resulted in two draws against sides whose associations had also declined FIFA's invitation. They were Germany, whom England played for the first time in an official game and drew 3-3 with in Berlin, and Austria, whom England drew 0-0 with in Vienna.

The following year, after sharing the Home Championship title with the Scots, England suffered a first defeat at the hands of the French,

in May 1931, going down 5-2 in Paris. In December 1931, Spain were the visitors to Highbury and England made amends for their defeat in Madrid with a crushing 7-1 win, despite the presence of Zamora in the Spanish goal. Jack Smith of Portsmouth, Thomas Johnson of Everton and Sammy Crooks of Derby County all scored twice, while Dean added another one to his England tally. England completed a fine season with a 3-0 defeat of the Scots at Wembley to take the 1931/32 Home Championship title.

England had begun playing official matches against European opponents in 1908, yet Austria's visit to England in December 1932, twenty-four years on, was only the fourth game England had played on home soil against Continental opposition. The previous three, two against Belgium and one against Spain, had resulted in easy wins, with England scoring 17 goals and conceding just 2. The Austrians, however, were a different prospect. England had managed to get a draw in Vienna eighteen months previously, but since then the Austrians had improved and were now dubbed the 'Wonder Team' of Europe. The match between the two sides was considered by many to be a showdown to decide who were the kings of European football. Despite the undoubted importance of the game, the Austrians were not given the opportunity to play at Wembley and the match was played at Stamford Bridge.

On the field it was a clash of styles. England had not long adopted a third back and the 'W' formation that was to become standard in English football. The Austrians, however, were the most skilful exponents of the tactic that saw their forwards attacking in a line with the support of their half-backs.

England won 4-3 in front of a 40,000 crowd but the deficiencies of their play were there for all to see. The Austrian approach was ahead of its time and, in hindsight, England's victory might have done a disservice to the longer-term development of its game. As one reporter put it: 'Though beaten [the Austrians] took the honours of the game by their quality. Only constant practice can produce such combination and deft control. Most certainly ball practice is quite a minor part of a footballer's training in England and teamwork is supposed to grow as naturally as wild flowers. What fallacies are these! Skill in any game is the reward of constant striving.'

In 1933, England played against three Continental sides. England's first match against Italy, in Rome, ended in a 1-1 draw while there were easy wins, 4-0 and 4-1 respectively, over Switzerland (again an inaugural contest) and France. However, these games were not being

Pre-match formalities as Blenkinsop introduces the guest of honour to the England team for the match against Scotland in April 1932. In line are: Waring, O'Dowd, Crooks (shaking hands), Strange, Barclay, Houghton, Pearson.

INTERNATIONAL MATCH

ENGLAND

VERSUS

AUSTRIA

AT

STAMFORD BRIDGE

Wednesday, 7th December, 1932

Kick-off 2.15 p.m.

Souvenir Programme   price 3ᵈ

A fine programme produced for the England v. Austria match at Stamford Bridge in 1932. England won an exciting game 4-3.

used by England as preparation for the second World Cup to be played in Italy the following year.

As in 1930, England remained in isolation and rejected FIFA's invitation. Thirty-two nations entered the tournament, which necessitated a qualifying programme to reduce the number of finalists to sixteen. Italy, Austria, Germany and Czechoslovakia, all of whom would have found England more than a handful, won through to the semi-finals. Italy beat Czechoslovakia 2-1 in the final and soon after their victory they were invited to London to take on England. The November 1934 game was billed in the English press as the unofficial play-off between the world's two best teams.

Although Italy had won the World Cup on their own soil they had won few friends around the world. Pressure from Mussolini meant that they had to win the tournament, at any cost, which led to some rather dubious tactics. However, the Italians' coach, Vittorio Pozzo, had spent time in England learning the English game and now he relished the chance to prove that his side was truly the best in the world by beating England in their own backyard.

The players chosen by the England selectors played for their clubs the Saturday before the game and, as a consequence, two of them – Derby County's right-back Thomas Cooper and Manchester City's centre forward Sam Tilson – had to withdraw through injury. Two Arsenal players, George Male and Ted Drake, both appearing in an England shirt for the first time, replaced them. These changes meant that seven of the eleven England players would come from the Highbury club, the hosts for the game. Arsenal, League champions and the dominant force in English football at that time, thus set a record that is unlikely to be equalled or beaten. With Eddie Hapgood, Arsenal's left-back, captaining the side, the complete line-up was as follows:

Moss (Arsenal), Male (Arsenal), Hapgood (Arsenal), Britton (Everton) Barker (Derby County), Copping (Arsenal), Matthews (Stoke City), Bowden (Arsenal), Drake (Arsenal), Bastin (Arsenal), Brook (Manchester City).

The game could have been one of the most memorable of all time for the right reasons, such

above: The England and France captains, Goodall and Delfour, in the pre-match ceremony at Tottenham in December 1933.

left: Sammy Crooks was a regular England selection during the early 1930s, gaining 26 caps.

was the skill on display and the desire of both teams to win. Instead, the match will always be remembered as the 'Battle of Highbury'.

England should have got off to a dream start when they were awarded a penalty after Ceresoli in the Italian goal had brought down Drake in the first minute of the game. However, the Italian goalkeeper atoned for his error by saving Eric Brook's firmly-struck shot. The incident set the tone for the rest of the 90 minutes. No sooner had the crowd digested England's missed opportunity than there was more controversy when Drake and Monti, a powerful and determined player of Argentine descent, clashed with the result that

Monti limped away from the challenge with a broken toe. He bravely struggled on for a few minutes but it became apparent that he could not be expected to complete the half, let alone the whole game, and so Pozzo pulled him off to avoid aggravating the injury.

The Italians, now down to ten men, were indignant about Drake's reckless challenge and they felt that the England player had deliberately injured Monti. The atmosphere between the two sides deteriorated further when Drake, again in the manner of a typical English centre forward, charged the Italian goalkeeper. The Italians' patience snapped and Monzeglio seized Drake by the neck. His

Two Arsenal stars, Hapgood (left) and Drake, who appeared for England in the 'Battle of Highbury' v. Italy in 1934.

actions went unpunished but England's early tactics had visibly unsettled the visitors.

Brook, making up for his missed penalty, headed home a Cliff Britton cross for England's first goal and then, within minutes, drove a twenty-yard free kick past the Italian goalkeeper for his second. Ceresoli in the Italian goal did not help his cause for the second England goal since he had confidently waved aside his defensive wall – believing that having already saved a spot kick from the Manchester City left-winger, twenty yards would be no problem.

The England captain, Hapgood, was then caught by a blow on the nose which forced him to leave the field. England responded with another goal from Drake and so, after only 15 minutes, the Italians found themselves 3-0 down. They were being run ragged and adopted spoiling tactics for the rest of the first half just to stay in the game. Each time an England forward looked like threatening the Italian goal he would be brought down. Amazingly, after an action-packed 45 minutes, England were beating the world champions 3-0.

Pozzo's side dramatically clawed their way back into the game in the second half with two goals from Meazza. The Highbury crowd was witnessing a fluent and at times breathtaking display from the Italians that was only occasionally flawed by outbursts of cynicism. England, with the young Stanley Matthews now marked out of the game, had no answer to the Italians, who had played for most of the match with just ten men. The home side spent much of the second half chasing shadows but they survived until the final whistle to win a dramatic game 3-2.

Nine England players had to receive treatment for injuries after the game but it is fair to say the home side had been just as much sinners – particularly in the early part of the game – as sinned against in the 'Battle of Highbury'. In the cold light of day it was probably only England's

physical approach in the opening quarter of the game that had given them the platform to beat the visitors, a fact which was not lost on the Italians who proclaimed a moral victory following their second-half performance. Indeed, England were indebted to the debutant Drake, who had burst onto the international scene with probably the most provocative first fifteen minutes of an England career of any of the thousand-plus footballers who have pulled on the England jersey before or since.

Following a poor Home Championship season in 1936/37, when they finished with just two points from their three games, England embarked

Eric Brook, seen here heading for goal, scored a brace to swing the 'Battle of Highbury' England's way.

on their first comprehensive tour to Scandinavia where they beat Norway 6-0, Sweden 4-0 and Finland 8-0. Freddie Steele of Stoke City, who celebrated his twenty-first birthday just days before the team left England, scored 7 of the 18 goals. However, the young striker's England career was to be short-lived since injury and competition from the incomparable Tommy Lawton restricted his appearances to just 6 games.

For the third time England refused to enter the World Cup and the FA arranged a three-match tour for England in the early summer of 1938 before the tournament started. The first of the games took the side to Berlin where they played a German side preparing for the World Cup, due to begin in France the following month. The Olympic Stadium was bursting to capacity and among the 115,000 crowd were three of the most senior members of the National Socialist government: Hess, Goebbels and Ribbentrop.

As the band struck up the German national anthem the England side gave the fascist salute, as requested by their hosts. There had been a heated exchange between the England players and match organizers before the game about the salute and one player, Stan Cullis, refused to conform to the request. As a consequence, the Wolves centre half was dropped from the side. The England team that did take the field lined up as follows:

Woodley (Chelsea), Sproston (Leeds United), Hapgood (Arsenal), Willingham (Huddersfield Town), Young (Huddersfield Town), Welsh (Charlton Athletic), Matthews (Stoke City), Robinson (Sheffield Wednesday), Broome (Aston Villa), Goulden (West Ham United), Bastin (Arsenal).

England's team versus Austria, Vienna, May 1936. From left to right: Sagar, Hobbis, Spence, Bastin, Male, Barker, Copping, Camsell, Bowden, Crayston, Hapgood. In a closely fought match Austria came out 2-1 winners, Camsell scoring for England.

Visibly uncomfortable at having been put through the experience of saluting the Nazis, the experience only served to spur on England's XI to produce one of the best performances of any England side at any time. The partisan atmosphere did not intimidate England but it did seem to put the Germans under extra strain as the game kicked-off. Goals were not long in coming. Cliff Bastin put England ahead on the quarter-hour, only to see the Germans equalize within five minutes. England, on top in these early stages, soon scored again as John Robinson restored their lead and then David Broome, on his debut, silenced the home crowd with England's third goal of the game. Matthews then weaved his way through the German defence for one of the all-time great England goals, beating three players before shooting past the goalkeeper to put England even further ahead. The Germans responded with a goal from a corner just before half-time to give themselves some hope.

Berliner Ausgabe

Berlin, Sonntag, 15. Mai 1938

BACHTER

Vor dem Länderspiel England—Deutschland, bei dem die Engländer 6:3 siegten
Während unserer Nationalhymnen hob die englische Mannschaft die Hand zum Deutschen Gruß

May 1938 and controversy raged over whether the team should give the Nazi salute in the Olympic Stadium in Berlin. Finally it was agreed that they should do so – the German press made much capital out of this acknowledgement of their leader by the English national side.

On the field it was a different story with England playing superbly to win 6-3. The programme for this memorable game is now a valuable collectors' item.

Following the break, a second from Robinson restored England's three-goal cushion. Although the German side refused to capitulate, any chance they may have had of turning the game round went when Len Goulden, winning his sixth cap, finished off the rout in fine style with a rasping shot that ripped the net away from the crossbar. The afternoon had begun in less than auspicious circumstances for England. It ended with the England side leaving the field with their heads held high and a 6-3 victory to savour. The rest of England's tour was an anti-climax, a defeat in Switzerland and a win in France failing to live up to that momentous day in Berlin.

Outside the home nations, 1938 meant another World Cup, in France. Sixteen countries made it to the finals but the Austrian team was forced to withdraw after Hitler's annexation and the Germans called up the best of the Austrian players to their own squad. In the modern era, such an act would have led FIFA to expel the aggressor nation from the tournament. But those were different

The final match of the 1938 European tour was in Paris, where a good England performance gave them a 4-2 victory. England's Bert Sproston is pictured taking flight to beat French defender Aston.

days and, with the finals on the horizon and one place in the last sixteen now unfilled, England were offered the vacant slot. The FA declined FIFA's invitation and the World Cup went ahead with fifteen teams. Germany were beaten in the first round after a replay against Switzerland. Italy beat the hosts, then Brazil and then Hungary in the final to be crowned worthy winners for the second time in succession.

Later that year, in October 1938, a FIFA Select side, including five Italians and two Germans, played England at Wembley to mark the FA's seventy-fifth anniversary. England beat this Rest of Europe team 3-0. England were now widely accepted to have one of the best sides in Europe and there was a distinct possibility that the FA would agree to participate in the next FIFA World Cup, in 1942, which many commentators felt England had

Brolly, the Irish defender, wins this heading duel with England's Joe Stephenson, of Leeds United, but the Irish team finished well beaten, 7-0, at Old Trafford in November 1938.

more than an even chance of winning. Such hopes were dashed in the autumn of 1939.

As the 1938/39 season came to a close and with the prospect of another European war looming, there was some anxiety about England's summer tour. However, the Foreign Office gave the FA the all-clear and England visited Italy, Yugoslavia and Romania, winning the final game after drawing in Milan and losing in Belgrade. On returning from the

tour, the FA deferred progress in arranging England's trip to Paris, scheduled for May 1940.

The international football played during the war was limited to one-off games between England, Scotland and Wales – there were no games against the Irish for the duration of the conflict – and all were classified as unofficial in the history of the game. There were some make-do-and-mend team selections along the way, but

England v Wales (Wartime Intl)
SAT. OCTOBER 25th 1941.   OFFICIAL PROGRAMME PRICE 3d.

BIRMINGHAM
FOOTBALL CLUB

H. MORRIS (*Chairman*)   *Directors :*   L. J. MORRIS
W. A. CAMKIN   D. WISEMAN   H. DARE.
                    J. WOOLMAN
Secretary : S. F. L. RICHARDS.   St. Andrew's Ground, Birmingham.

This afternoon we welcome to the battle-scarred St. Andrew's Ground the representatives and officials of the English and Welsh Football Associations, their distinguished guests, and the players and officials engaged in the Match. St. Andrew's has not previously been chosen for an International. On a particular morning last November, a gathering such as to-day's would have been hard to imagine, but thanks to many willing helpers and the efforts of Secretary S. F. L. Richards—who has made the arrangements without in any way interfering with his whole time A.F.S. duties—many difficulties have been overcome.

The Prime Minister's presence and that of other members of the War Cabinet, at Wembley three weeks ago, testified to the fact that a limited amount of relaxation is essential to the Nation's War Effort. A rousing game this afternoon will be a tonic for next week's "production" efforts.

We congratulate our players, "Billy" Hughes and Donald Dearson in once more representing their country this afternoon. Frankly, a Welsh team without a "Blues" player would look a little strange. Congratulations also to Fred Harris (England Reserve) and W. Kendrick (Welsh Team Trainer).

AIR RAID PRECAUTIONS.

In the event of an air raid warning during the Match, spectators are requested to carry out instructions which will at once be communicated over the loud speakers. Those wishing to leave the Ground to proceed direct to their homes may do so, but should not use the street shelters in the vicinity of the Ground.

above: Captains Matt Busby and Stan Cullis shake hands prior to the England *v.* Scotland game at Wembley, February 1944.

left: The outbreak of war in 1939 brought a halt to official matches. Games that were played were staged at various venues around the country. The programme shown illustrates some of the prevailing conditions and the need to advise the spectators of air raid precautions.

there were also some great games played in front of some amazingly large crowds by the biggest names in world football.

The first wartime international took place in Cardiff, in November 1939. England were the visitors, drawing 1-1 with Wales in front of a 28,000 crowd. The game also marked England's first ever use of a substitute when Jim Lewis came on for Joe Bacuzzi.

In the spring of 1940, England played two games. The first, against Wales, was the first time the Welsh had ever played at Wembley. A crowd of 40,000 saw the visitors defeat England 1-0, an indication that throughout the war years it would be the Welsh rather than the Scots who would often present England with their sternest tests.

A crowd of 75,000 turned up for the Scotland v. England game at Hampden Park in May 1940. They were clearly not deterred by unconfirmed reports that the German Luftwaffe were planning on bombing the event. This rumour prevented England's goalkeeper, Sam Bartram, from appearing, the RAF refusing him leave to play in the game. His place was taken by Frank Woodley of Chelsea, while the game ended in the 1-1 draw.

England played six games in 1941, then five in each year between 1942 and 1944. In 1945, they played a sixth match, just weeks after VE Day, when the French were invited to London for a

above: Scotland visited Wembley five times during the war years (the other games being played at St James' Park, Old Trafford and Villa Park). The game in October 1944 saw Goulden slip this shot past Cumming in the Scots' goal – one of six England scored against the two from Scotland.

right: Programme for the Victory international, England v. France. The wartime allies drew 2–2.

Victory game. An exuberant 60,000 spectators came to Wembley to see the 2-2 draw.

With many of the top players playing in other representative games at the end of the war, England appeared just four times in 1946. They beat Belgium 2-0 at Wembley, lost 1-0 at Hampden Park, beat Switzerland 4-1 at Stamford Bridge and then lost 2-1 in Paris against France.

In total, England played 36 wartime matches, including the 6 Victory games that celebrated the end of the conflict, winning 22, drawing 6 and losing 8. Stanley Matthews played in the most games (29), while Tommy Lawton appeared 23 times, scoring 24 goals. Stan Cullis played in 20 matches and would have played in more but for a broken leg. Matthews, Lawton and Cullis were three England players who were lucky to have international careers that straddled the war, but others were less fortunate.

Seventy-five professional footballers playing in England before the war died in action. One Arsenal player, Herbie Roberts, had been capped once by England, in the 1931 game against Scotland. Roberts was one of two England internationals to die in active service. The other was Leeds United's Joseph Stephenson, who had played twice for his country before the war, against Scotland in 1938 and Northern Ireland in 1939.

EDDIE HAPGOOD
Arsenal
Left-back
30 international caps (1933-1939)

Hapgood made his debut for England in the 'Battle of Highbury' against Italy in 1933. He was virtually a permanent selection until the outbreak of hostilities in 1939 and he would have gained many more caps but for the war. Many football historians credit him for being the first 'football-playing' full-back – coupling great tackling ability with a fine football brain. He was captain in 21 of his international matches.

STANLEY MATTHEWS
Stoke City/Blackpool
Outside right
54 international caps (1934-1957)

An England international first selected in 1934 at the age of nineteen, he was still in the team in 1957 – bridging twenty-three years and setting a record that is unlikely to be overtaken. Add around 30 wartime selections to his tally and the testimony to Matthew's remarkable talents are obvious. An entertainer and a football genius, he was nicknamed the 'Wizard of the Dribble'. He only scored some 11 goals during his international career but he orchestrated many more. Although often brought down by frustrated full-backs, he never retaliated. In 1965 he became the first footballer to receive a (much-deserved) knighthood for services to football.

FOREVER
ENGLAND

In 1946 the Football Association appointed Walter Winterbottom as England's team coach. He retained that role for some sixteen years covering 139 matches, winning 78 and drawing 33 of those games.

The British associations rejoined FIFA in 1946. At the same time, the FA appointed an England team manager for the very first time. They chose Walter Winterbottom, a man with an impeccable reputation as a first-class administrator and coach. He had trained as a teacher before embarking on a football career, playing centre half for Manchester United. The war brought a premature end to his playing career and he joined the RAF.

England's first fixtures after the war, in September 1946, took the side across the Irish Sea for games against Northern Ireland and the Republic of Ireland, in Belfast and Dublin respectively. The game against Northern Ireland was the first of the Home Championship series, while the game in Dublin was England's first against an Irish side that was not considered 'British'. The match represented a political landmark between the two countries and was marked by a post-match reception held by the Irish prime minister, Eamonn de Valera. The England XI for both games was as follows:

Swift (Manchester City), Scott (Arsenal), Hardwick (Middlesbrough), Wright (Wolverhampton Wanderers), Franklin (Stoke City), Cockburn (Manchester United), Finney (Preston North End), Carter (Derby City), Lawton (Chelsea), Mannion (Middlesbrough), Langton (Blackburn Rovers).

From this XI, only Horatio Carter and Tommy Lawton had pulled on an England shirt before the war. Carter was unquestionably one of England's all-time great playmakers and also scored more than his fair share of goals. His England career recommenced following a ten-year gap when he stepped out to play Northern Ireland, but he wasted no time in getting his name onto the scoresheet, putting England into the lead in the very first minute of the game.

Tommy Lawton, more than many other England players of his era, could be justified in saying that the war had ripped the heart out of his internatonal career. Before the war Lawton had

Left to right: Tommy Lawton, Raich Carter, Wilf Mannion and Frank Swift.

Tommy Lawton of Chelsea and Raich Carter of Derby County were two fine players, whose careers were interrupted by the war. Between them, however, they still managed to collect 36 caps plus many more in unofficial internationals played during the hostilities. The winner of 26 caps between 1947 and 1952, Wilf Mannion, a

one-club man at Middlesbrough, was a talented playmaker for both club and country. Frank Swift's best years were lost to the Second World War. He was first selected in 1946, by which time he was thirty-three years old. His international career ended in 1949 with 19 caps plus many wartime appearances. He became a press reporter and he died in the Munich Air Disaster in 1958. He was a truly great goalkeeper.

become the youngest player, at nineteen, to score for England. The war deprived him of England caps but it did not deprive him of his goal scoring instincts as he carried on scoring for England at the rate of a goal a game until his final cap in 1948. That match against Northern Ireland marked his ninth appearance for his country. He celebrated it with a goal – his seventh for England – in the 7-2 win in Belfast.

Wilf Mannion hit a hat-trick on his debut in the game to become the third England player to achieve the feat since the turn of the century. The honour of captaining England for their first game after the war fell to George Hardwick. Although he had played a number of times for England during the war, he had

not represented his country before it and went on to gain a unique record of 13 England caps in official internationals, all as captain.

While Northern Ireland had proved to be weak opponents, the Republic's side was made of sterner stuff and effectively contained England, limiting the visitors to a 1-0 win thanks to a Tom Finney goal. That season, England went on to win the Home Championship following a 3-0 win over Wales and a 1-1 draw with the Scots.

England hit a purple patch over the next couple of years, dominating the Home Championship and beating other European sides with, at times, quite considerable ease: Holland 8-2, Portugal 10-0, Belgium 5-2, Italy 4-0 in Turin and

The England team (suitably capped) for the game against Wales in November 1948. From left to right, back row: Leuty, Scott, Aston, Winterbottom (manager), Swift, Wright, Ward, Bourne (trainer). Front row: Matthews, Mortensen, Milburn, Shackleton, Finney, Franklin.

Action from the first post-war international at Wembley. Neil Franklin is challenged by Jimmy Delaney after Frank Swift failed to hold a Scottish cross. The match ended as a 1-1 draw.

Switzerland 6-0. The only major blot on the landscape came in September 1949 when the Republic of Ireland beat England 2-0 at Goodison Park, so becoming the first foreign side to beat England in England. The game against Belgium marked a milestone for England when Jimmy Mullen came on as England's first-ever substitute in an official game. The Wolves outside left, whose England career revolved around the availability of the incomparable Finney, also scored in that game.

England were the uncrowned kings of European football and Stanley Matthews, Tommy Lawton, Jackie Milburn, Stan Mortensen and Tom Finney were the stars of the show whenever they performed in the white shirts of England. Finney, affectionately known as the 'Preston Plumber', scored twice against the pre-war world champions Italy, and later recalled that display as 'the finest performance by any team I played for'.

The return of the British to FIFA meant that for the first time the home countries would take part in the World Cup. FIFA generously decided that the 1949/50 Home Championship campaign would double as a qualifying group for the 1950 World Cup and that the top two sides would qualify for the finals in Brazil.

Scotland opened the group with an emphatic 8-2 win in Belfast against a hapless Northern Ireland. England then beat Wales 4-1 in Cardiff with a hat-trick from Milburn following an opener from Mortensen. Scotland beat Wales 2-0 and then England demolished Northern Ireland 9-2.

With England and Scotland both on maximum points, with two wins from two games, as the final group match approached both had qualified for Brazil. However, astonishingly, the Scottish FA had stated that if they were to finish in second place behind England they would refuse the invitation to go to Brazil. So, instead of the

Stanley Matthews turns Scotland's George Young at Hampden Park.

encounter at Hampden Park being a celebration of both countries' qualification, it was turned into a crucial, sudden-death game.

The England selectors decided to leave out Matthews, preferring Chelsea's Roy Bentley as a foil for Mortensen and Mannion. It was a tactical change that looked risky but which paid dividends as England dominated the game. Scotland were left to look for openings on the break but made little impact against England's full-back pairing of Tottenham Hotspur's Alf Ramsey and John Aston of Manchester United.

England took the lead midway through the second half with a goal from Bentley and comfortably withheld all the pressure the Scots could muster to win, duly qualifying for Brazil as British champions. Scotland stubbornly confirmed their initial decision not to go, despite protests from their own and even England's players.

The programme for the crunch match with Scotland. Who would qualify for the 1950 World Cup in South America?

Alf Ramsey, who would ultimately lead England to greater things, was first capped as a Southampton player but moved to Tottenham in 1950, where he earned 31 of his 32 caps.

1950 WORLD CUP QUALIFYING GROUP ONE FINAL TABLE

	P	W	D	L	GF	GA	P
England	3	3	0	0	14	3	6
Scotland	3	2	0	1	10	3	4
Wales	3	0	1	2	1	6	1
N. Ireland	3	0	1	2	4	17	1

The Scots were not the only nation to qualify for the finals and not take part: Portugal, Argentina, Czechoslovakia and Turkey all pulled out. The USSR and Hungary, both world-class football nations, also refused to take part in the competition. So, in reality, the World Cup finals of 1950 were severely devalued as a contest to find the best team in the world as many of the best, including the disqualified Germans, were missing.

When the pool matches were drawn just prior to the tournament itself, two more countries, India – who had qualified for the finals without playing a game – and France, both withdrew when they saw how far they would have to travel when in Brazil. So just thirteen countries took part in the tournament, which by now was in a state of shambles.

For England, the most fancied of the European sides, the 1950 World Cup was to be a disaster, despite setting out for Brazil with a series of fine results under their belts. They had beaten France 3-1 in Paris and the Italians 2-0 at White Hart Lane. Portugal were despatched 5-3 and Belgium 4-1 as part of a seven-game winning streak, a run that had seen England net 28 goals. Winterbottom took a squad of world-famous stars with him to South America but, in just a few short days at the end of June 1950, justified confidence turned to despair and embarrassment. The England party must have wished that they, like the Scots, had stayed at home.

England were favourites to clinch the one place from their group of four, their opponents being Spain, Chile and the USA. Their first game in World Cup finals was in Rio against Chile. In the Chile side was the Newcastle United centre forward, George Robledo, their only full-time professional. The England side was:

> Williams (Wolverhampton Wanderers),
> Ramsey (Tottenham Hotspur), Aston
> (Manchester United), Wright (Wolverhampton
> Wanderers), Hughes (Liverpool), Dickenson
> (Portsmouth), Finney (Preston North End),
> Mannion (Middlesbrough), Bentley (Chelsea),
> Mortensen (Blackpool), Mullen
> (Wolverhampton Wanderers).

England had little experience of playing under such heavy climatic conditions and looked lacklustre. They failed to impress. However, one goal in each half, first from Mortensen, then from Mannion, saw them safely through their first group match.

Bert Williams watches as the USA's winning goal is scored by Gaetjens during England's first-round defeat at the World Cup finals.

England's next opponents were the USA. Managed by a Scotsman, Bill Jeffrey, and captained by Eddie McIlvenny, once of Wrexham and one of three non-US-born players in the side, they had proved to be more than a handful against Spain in their first game and were unlucky to lose 3-1. Just one England selector, Arthur Drewry, travelled with the side and it was his decision to pick the same XI who had beaten the Chileans. There was no place for Matthews, who Winterbottom had wanted in the side, but the England coach decided not to argue the point – Matthews would be saved for the more important games ahead.

A small crowd of just over 10,000 settled into their seats at the Mineiro Stadium in Belo Horizonte, a town 300 miles north of Rio. As the game got underway all seemed to be going to plan as England pressurized the American goal with a number of opportunities narrowly missing their target. However, with just eight minutes left of the first half, and England growing increasingly frustrated at the dogged defending of the Americans and the heroics of their goalkeeper Frank Borghi, the incredible happened. Barely out of their own half thus far, the Americans broke free from their shackles. Walter Bahr drove a shot in from the left, which Wolves' Bert Williams seemed to have covered. Joe Gaetjens popped up to deflect the ball past the diving England goalkeeper and put his side into an undeserved lead.

Although England piled on the pressure in the second half, claiming an equalizer through a Jimmy Mullin header which the Italian referee adjudged had not crossed the line, the Americans also threatened to extend their lead, catching an increasingly desperate England on the break on a number of occasions. It was not to be England's day and at the final whistle they skulked off to their dressing room, red-faced, leaving a team of Americans and a crowd of Brazilians to celebrate the most unlikely of results.

To England's dismay, Spain beat Chile 2-0 and now they faced a mountainous task to stay in the competition. They had to beat Spain by four clear goals to qualify for the second phase. Matthews and Milburn returned to the side while two others, Blackburn Rovers left-back Bill Eckersley and Tottenham inside-left Eddie Baily, were given debuts as England went for broke. The game was held back in the Maracana in Rio and the crowd of nearly 75,000 was the biggest of the tournament, excluding the massive crowds of twice this figure that crammed into the Maracana whenever the home team played.

Losing 0-1 is not the end of the world, but it seemed like it to English fans when the USA won at Belo Horizonte in the 1950 World Cup. Goalscorer Joe Gaetjens is chaired off the field.

England started the game with spirit, restoring some battered pride. Playing some good football in a goalless first half, they had what seemed to be a perfectly good strike by Milburn disallowed by the Italian referee. Their mission was still possible at the interval, but became insurmountable just four minutes after the break when Spain scored. England were seen to visibly wilt and never got back into their stride. The final whistle was a relief to many in the England camp – the torture was over, they had lost and one of the pre-tournament favourites were out.

The press rounded on the culprits. Not the players, nor the manager, England's failure was blamed on the rigours of the domestic game and the mismanagement of the tournament by FIFA. The Sunday Pictorial summed up the feelings of most, 'What can you expect? The players had been in constant competition since August 1949. Why did the FA take on a gruelling continental tour a short head away from the Latin American excursion? The time spent travelling on planes and trains is not worth a pinch of powdered owl food compared with time in bed. From South America came disturbing reports that our team had not slept while always on the move.'

1950 WORLD CUP POOL TWO FINAL TABLE

	P	W	D	L	GF	GA	P
Spain	3	3	0	0	6	1	6
England	3	1	0	2	2	2	2
Chile	3	1	0	2	5	6	2
USA	3	1	0	2	4	8	2

Argentina become the first non-British team to play an official international at Wembley, losing in May 1951 by 2 goals to 1. Here, Mortensen heads past Argentine goalkeeper Rugilo to score England's first.

Four sides qualified for the second phase, which was played on a league basis with all four teams – Brazil, Uruguay, Sweden and Spain – playing each other. Brazil breezed past the Europeans, scoring 13 goals in two games. Uruguay drew with Spain and then beat Sweden to set up a 'final' more by luck than judgement; the Brazil versus Uruguay match just happened to be scheduled as the last of the group matches. An incredible 200,000 spectators descended on the Maracana stadium and witnessed one of the best games in the history of the World Cup. Most had come expecting to celebrate a Brazilian victory but they left in admiration of a fine performance from the Uruguayans, particularly from their centre half and captain, Valera, who turned in an heroic performance in the 2-1 win.

The England manager, the selectors and players survived the muted backlash to their disappointing World Cup debut and, to their credit, the England team bounced right back into top form and, from October 1950 until November 1953, lost just twice in 25 games.

In May 1951, Argentina came to England and became the first nation other than the Scots to play at Wembley in an official match. Over the years, games between the two have produced some of the most nail-biting and controversial moments in England's football history. This first encounter was no exception as England had to come from behind to win 2-1 and preserve their unbeaten home record in games against opposition from outside the British Isles. For much of the game it looked as though the South Americans, inspired by winger Labruna-Lousta and goalkeeper Rugilo, would pull-off a shock win. However, Mortensen proved England's saviour by scoring twice (although the second goal looked suspiciously offside) to win the game and take his personal goal tally for England up to 22 in just 23 appearances.

The 1951 team that played Wales at Ninian Park, drawing 1-1. From left to right, back row: Lofthouse, Ramsey, Williams, Barass, Dickenson, L. Smith. Front row: Finney, Thompson, Wright, Baily, Medley.

Two weeks later England played Portugal at Goodison Park and included one new cap in the side. Tottenham's right-back Bill Nicholson pulled on an England shirt for the first time as a replacement for Billy Wright. Nicholson had a dream start to his international career. In his own words, 'We kicked off, the ball came to me and I lobbed it forward. Stan Pearson nodded it back and I ran on to let go a first time shot which, from the moment I hit it, I knew was going in.' However, for the man who was to achieve greatness as manager of Tottenham's double-winning side, his debut goal for England after 19 seconds of international football was to be the highlight of an international career which was to last just 90 minutes. England won 5-2 but Nicholson was not picked again.

In May 1952, after sharing the Home Championship with Wales and winning in Glasgow, England embarked on a three-match tour of Europe. The first, against Italy in Florence, was a poor game and ended in a 1-1 draw, with some players making muffled comments as to the length of the domestic season which had left them jaded and unable to give their best for their country.

England drew 1-1 with Italy in Florence in 1952. In the pre-match hype, the Italian press cast Italy as David and England in the role of Goliath.

Winterbottom and his squad then moved on to Vienna to play the crack Austrian side, who had lost only 2 of their previous 16 games; they had scored no fewer than 57 goals in those matches, hitting eight past Belgium and seven past Yugoslavia and, most significantly for England, had out-classed Scotland 4-0 just the year before.

England's improved form since the aberration of the 1950 World Cup gave the game added spice, as it was recognized across the continent as the unofficial champions of Europe showdown. Since the end of the war, Austria had been occupied by Allied forces and a large number of English soldiers were given leave to attend the game thus, for the first time, giving a travelling England side the sort of support they had never had before. England lined up in Vienna as follows:

Merrick (Birmingham City), Ramsey (Tottenham Hotspur), Eckersley (Blackburn Rovers), Wright (Wolverhampton Wanderers), Froggatt (Portsmouth), Dickenson (Portsmouth), Finney (Preston North End), Sewell (Sheffield Wednesday), Lofthouse (Bolton Wanderers), Baily (Tottenham Hotspur), Elliott (Burnley).

In international terms it was an experienced side, most of whom had been to Brazil two years before. There was no more experienced player on show than England's captain, Billy Wright, who was playing his 42nd international (thereby breaking Bob Crompton's long-standing England record). However, there were question marks over the potency of a forward line that was made up of players who had averaged a little over ten goals each during the previous League season.

The opening phase of the match raised the fears of the England supporters. Austria looked sharp, fast and effective in attack, whereas England created few opportunities to trouble Musil's goal. However, against the run of play Eddie Baily won the ball on the halfway line and found Billy Elliott who in turn found Jackie Sewell. With the Austrian defence back-pedalling, Sewell's cross was volleyed home by Lofthouse to give the red-shirted Englishmen a 1-0 lead.

Before the visitors had time to savour it, the Austrians hit back as Jack Froggatt brought down Dienst, allowing Huber the chance to level the scores from the penalty spot, which he did. Again there was little time to digest the new scoreline before Froggatt, atoning for his reckless challenge seconds before, began an England counter-attack from deep in his own half. It was Froggatt to

Tom Finney was often compared to Matthews – but that was unfair to both players. Both were world class, while Finney was probably a better all-round player, selected at left-wing and on occasions at centre forward for England. Between 1947 and 1959 he won 76 caps and scored 30 goals.

Wright, Wright to Sewell, then Sewell shimmied before shooting low and hard with his right foot into the net – England's lead was restored. Even then, with three goals already scored, the first-half action was not yet over and with just a couple of minutes remaining before the break, Dienst for once shrugged off the challenge of Wright to beat Gil Merrick and level the scores at 2-2.

By contrast, the second half was a tougher, tighter battle with neither side allowing their opponents the space to bear down on goal. That was until the 82nd minute. The Austrians had won

a corner, the cross came in but Merrick rose to grab the ball cleanly. Spotting Finney, the England goalkeeper set his winger free with a quick throw. Lofthouse had begun a run into the Austrian half and Finney found him with a perfect ball, which split what remained of the Austrian defence. Musil advanced but checked, that split-second hesitation costing the Austrian goalkeeper the yard that Lofthouse needed. Goalkeeper and centre forward clattered into each other. Lofthouse was laid out but the ball rolled past them both and into the Austrian net. The Lion of

England *v.* Belgium in 1952 and Merrick saves from Mermans whilst Smith and Froggatt cover.

Vienna had got that vital last touch and England were back in the lead at 3-2.

The game restarted with England's hero off the field and receiving treatment but he soon returned to the fray only to be denied a hat-trick as a shot cracked against a post. The cushion of a two-goal lead was not needed. England had burst the Austrian bubble and at the final whistle had secured a famous victory.

A 2-2 draw with the Scots ensured a share of the Home Championship title with Scotland in the 1952/53 season. England, now viewed by many across the continent as the best in Europe, then set out for South America to exorcize the ghost of their failure at the World Cup in 1950.

Their first game on the tour was against Argentina in Buenos Aires, but heavy rain caused the match to be abandoned after 23 minutes without a goal being scored. England then moved on to Santiago to face the Chileans. Here, Lofthouse and Manchester United's Tommy Taylor scored the goals in a 2-1 win. However, England's third game, against world champions Uruguay, ended in a 2-1 defeat. England returned home via

November 1953 and Billy Wright leads England out at Wembley for the infamous match against Hungary, led by their captain Puskas.

New York, where they beat the USA 6-3 in a game to celebrate the Coronation of Queen Elizabeth II. This game, at the Yankee Stadium, was also noteworthy in that it was the first England had ever played under floodlights.

At the start of the 1953/54 season, England beat Wales 4-1 and then shared eight goals with a FIFA Select side. Their next opponents, in November 1953, were Hungary, a side that had grown in reputation since their victory at the 1952 Olympics. This was the Hungarians' first game at Wembley and the first between the sides since before the war when England dominated the encounters between the two countries, losing just once in five games. England fielded the nucleus of a strong side but used the friendly to blood two new caps, Blackpool's inside right Ernie Taylor and the Spurs outside left, amateur George Robb. Robb owed his inclusion to a sustained press campaign but, for both players, the game was to be their first and last in an England shirt.

The match got off to a cracking start as the Hungarians' short, swift passing movements left the England defence standing: Bozsik, Zakarias and then Hidgekuti combined for the latter to score in the very first minute of the game.

Hidgekuti then beat Merrick for a second time, only to see his 'goal' ruled out for offside. England drew level with a goal from Sewell, but 1-1 became 1-2 before the game was more than 20 minutes old, when Hidgekuti added a second for the visitors. Then enter Puskas – latching on to a cross from the right, the gifted Magyar buried the ball in the back of the England net to increase his side's lead. Puskas then tapped home the Hungarians' fourth and England's proud record of never being beaten at home by a foreign side was looking decidedly under threat. It was not just the scoreline, now 4-1, but the sheer skill and total domination of the Magyars that left the crowd mesmerized. A team out of their league was outplaying England.

Mortensen pulled one back for England – his last goal in what was to be, like others in the England team that day, his final appearance for his country – but this only served to spur on the Hungarians. Bozsik added a fifth and Hidgekuti completed his hat-trick with a fine volley from a Puskas lob. Ramsey got his third international goal, from the penalty spot, but England were well beaten. The inquests began as the final whistle blew: England 3 Hungary 6.

This was England's first defeat at Wembley by a non-British side. Although they had played just 21 internationals at home against opposition from outside the British Isles prior to this game, the fall-out from it was to be great and long-lasting. The recent defeats at the hands of the Republic of Ireland in 1949 and the USA in 1950 were both seen as one-off setbacks. The defeat at the hands of the Hungarians at Wembley overshadowed these and all the others in England's history up to this time. It was incontrovertible now that England

November 1953, England 3 Hungary 6. England's first defeat on home soil. From left to right: Eckersley, Merrick, Johnson and Hidgekuti 'scoring'.

was not the force in world football that it thought it was.

Luckily, England's route to the 1954 World Cup finals had been secured just days before the Hungarian humiliation, when England beat Northern Ireland 3-1 at Goodison Park. For the second tournament running FIFA had been generous in allowing the British associations to provide two finalists. With Scotland and Wales sharing six goals in a 3-3 draw, England's victory over the Irish, after already beating Wales 4-1, qualified them for Switzerland. This time, unlike in 1950, the Scots agreed to accept the invitation held out to the second-placed side and so the game between the two in Glasgow, which England won 4-2, was less fraught than the contest four years previously.

above: Lofthouse heads for goal while Finney and Taylor look on in the thrilling 4-4 draw with Belgium, 1954.

left: Ferenc Puskas (Hungary) presents Billy Wright with a bouquet prior to presenting England with a 7-1 thrashing in Budapest, May 1954.

1954 WORLD CUP QUALIFYING GROUP THREE FINAL TABLE

	P	W	D	L	GF	GA	P
England	3	3	0	0	11	4	6
Scotland	3	1	1	1	8	8	3
N. Ireland	3	1	0	2	4	7	2
Wales	3	0	1	2	5	9	1

Winterbottom's side prepared for the finals with a two-match trip to Yugoslavia and Hungary, both of whom had also qualified for the finals. For England, the warm-up games did little to build any self-belief. They lost 1-0 in Belgrade and were then demolished 7-1 in Budapest – England's worst-ever defeat. Hungary were the tournament's red-hot favourites but there was little consolation in that for the English.

Thus it was a dispirited England side that took the field against Belgium for their first pool game of the 1954 Swiss World Cup. England's opponents had provided them with an easy win at Wembley a little over eighteen months previously when Burnley's outside left, Elliot, and Lofthouse both netted twice in a 5-0 win, but these were now different days for the England side. The selectors had, perhaps surprisingly, decided to keep the same defensive formation that had caved in against the Hungarians in Budapest but shook up the attack that took the field in the St Jakob Stadium, Basle, in front of 14,000 spectators.

It was a strategy that looked like backfiring on England as they succumbed to an early goal from the Belgians. However, there was to be no capitulation this time from England, and Matthews, who had been rested for the second Hungary match,

The England team line up for the anthems prior to the match against Belgium at the 1954 World Cup finals. From left to right: Wright, Merrick, Staniforth, Dickenson, Owen, Matthews, Broadis, Taylor, Finney, Lofthouse, Byrne.

proved to be every bit as good as the considerable reputation that still went before him and inspired England to a 3-1 lead. Ivor Broadis and Lofthouse scored before the break and then, just after the hour mark, Broadis added his second.

At 3-1 up England looked to be cruising but the Belgians hit back with two goals to send the match into extra time. Lofthouse restored England's advantage in the first period but his side failed yet again to hold onto a lead and the game finished in a 4-4 draw. It was a frustrating display and after the game the thirty-nine-year-old Matthews, who had given a faultless display as the winger-provider *par excellence*, referred to some of his team-mates saying that 'they had thrown the game away'.

As they only had to play two of the three teams in the group, England avoided the Italians but had to play, and beat, the host nation Switzerland to qualify for the second phase of the competition. England had to reorganize due to injuries to Matthews and centre half, Syd Owen. Captain Wright moved into the centre of the midfield to make way for Huddersfield Town's Bill McGarry, while the Wolves pair of inside left Dennis Wilshaw and outside left Jimmy Mullen also came into the side, which took the field without Lofthouse.

The game attracted a partisan crowd of over 43,000, but they left disappointed. England proved to be the stronger of the two teams, drawing on their greater experience to control the game and, crucially, take the chances they were presented with. Mullen and Wilshaw scored one each as England claimed a place in the quarter-finals with their best result in two World Cup tournaments.

1954 WORLD CUP POOL FOUR FINAL TABLE

	P	W	D	L	GF	GA	P
England	2	1	1	0	6	4	3
Italy	2	1	0	1	5	3	2
Switzerland	2	1	0	1	2	3	2
Belgium	2	0	1	1	5	8	1

Play-off: Switzerland 4 Italy 1

England's quarter-final opponents were Uruguay. The game was to be one of the most entertaining of the whole tournament – this was no mean feat as the scores from the other quarter-finals read: Austria 7 Switzerland 5, Hungary 4 Brazil 2, West Germany 2 Yugoslavia 0.

England strengthened their side, bringing back Matthews and Lofthouse for Tommy Taylor and Mullen. But it was the South Americans who took an early lead through Borges. Matthews, again inspirational, then set Dennis Wilshaw free to provide Lofthouse with an opportunity to level the scores. The big centre forward duly capitalized. However, shortly before the break, a mistake from Merrick allowed the South Americans to restore their one-goal advantage.

England began the second half well but failed to turn their superior possession into goals. Against the run of play, and as a result of some poor goalkeeping from Merrick, the South Americans increased their lead. Finney pulled one back for England after 67 minutes, which heralded a spell of intense England pressure, but

the Uruguayans held out and killed off the game with a fourth goal just twelve minutes before the end. Although defeated 4-2 and out of the tournament, England's overall performance at the finals had helped restore a little of the lost pride of the previous campaign.

Hungary disposed of the Uruguayans in their semi-final to face the unfancied West Germans in the final. The two teams had met in the opening phase of the tournament, a game that the Hungarians had won 8-3. However, the Germans were to be no pushovers this time. From a 2-2 scoreline at half-time the Germans scored the winner with just six minutes remaining to become the first unseeded side to win the World Cup.

One of the main casualties of England's lukewarm performance at the Swiss World Cup was the Birmingham City goalkeeper, Merrick, who never added to his 23 caps. In his place the selectors plumped for the Manchester United's Ray Wood, a 'keeper renowned for his exceptional courage and an air of confidence that it was hoped he would instil in those playing in front of him. Wood came in for the two Home Championship fixtures against Northern Ireland and Wales in the autumn of 1954.

England won both games with the Manchester City inside forward Don Revie and the Fulham centre forward Johnny Haynes scoring on their international debuts in the 2-0 win in Belfast. The visit of Wales to Wembley saw Roy Bentley grab a hat-trick in his first game in three years for England, the match ending in a 3-2 win for England.

The world champions, West Germany, were England's next opponents, in late 1954. It was the first time England had played a German side since the war and, despite the visitors' status as holders of the Jules Rimet trophy, the Wembley crowd were expectant of an England win. With just two changes from the side that had beaten the Welsh the month before, England turned in a fine performance. Goals from Bentley, Ron Allen and Len Shackleton saw the team record a convincing 3-1 victory.

England then completed a four-match winning sequence and took the Home Championship title in April 1955 with a thumping 7-2 victory over the Scots, surprisingly England's first win over the

right: December 1954 saw West Germany play their first match in Britain since the war: Wright and Joseph Posipal exchange pennants.

below: December 1954 saw England defeat West Germany 3-1 at Wembley. Roy Bentley and Bill Slater are on the attack.

old enemy at Wembley in an official international since before the war. The hero of the day was Dennis Wilshaw, who hit four of the goals. Lofthouse added two more and Revie completed the rout.

1954/55 HOME CHAMPIONSHIP FINAL TABLE

	P	W	D	L	GF	GA	P
England	3	3	0	0	12	4	6
Scotland	3	1	1	1	5	9	3
Wales	3	1	0	2	5	6	2
N. Ireland	3	0	1	2	4	7	1

A three-match summer tour at the end of the 1954/55 season saw England lose 1-0 to France in Paris before drawing 1-1 in Madrid against the Spanish. The game was played at the cavernous Bernabeu stadium and attracted a huge crowd of 128,000 – an attendance which remains England's highest outside the Maracana and Hampden Park. In the final game of the tour, England went down 3-1 in Oporto against the Portuguese.

The following season, 1955/56, all four home countries shared the domestic title for the first time in its sixty-one-year history. England drew 1-1 with Scotland in Glasgow. In the team that day was Reg Matthews of Coventry City, then a Third Division club. Matthews became the first player from outside the top two divisions to debut in the showpiece game of the season. Fifteen others had been capped for England while playing for Third Division sides since the lower league was formed in 1920, but few exceeded Matthews' tally as he added another four caps in later years. However, the highlight of the

Programme for the Spain v. England match played in Madrid in 1955. The game ended as a 1-1 draw.

international season was the first visit to Wembley of Brazil, in May 1956. The South Americans succumbed to the magic of Stanley Matthews and two goals each from Tommy Taylor and Colin Grainger helped England to a 4-2 win.

The 1958 World Cup loomed. England's qualifying group comprised the Republic of Ireland and Denmark. England's confidence was high and, with a rare piece of foresight, the FA organized a three-match tour in May 1956 that took in Sweden, Finland and West Germany.

May 1956 saw the Brazilians visit Wembley. The South Americans were defeated 4-2. This photograph shows a Tommy Taylor header that was saved by Gylmar.

May 1956 and Nat Lofthouse scores England's fourth goal against Finland in the 5-1 win in Helsinki.

A 0-0 draw in Stockholm was followed by an easy 5-1 win in Helsinki. England then went to Berlin to face the Germans, who were looking to avenge their drubbing at Wembley, but England again conquered and came away 3-1 victors against the world champions for the second time in eighteen months.

England began their 1958 World Cup qualification campaign against Denmark at Molineux. The England number nine, Taylor, helped himself to a hat-trick and his Old Trafford club-mate Duncan Edwards added two more in an easy 5-2 win. Taylor scored another three at Wembley

against the Irish as England won 5-1 and then followed that with two in the 4-1 win in Copenhagen. The Republic had beaten Denmark twice, but maximum points from three games for England meant that they needed only to draw the final match of the group, in Dublin, to be assured of qualification. However, all did not go to plan as the Irish took a surprise 1-0 lead. England needed a goal from Bristol City's John Atyeo in the last minute of the game to stop the two sides playing-off for a place in Sweden. Although the result was important for England, the game also marked the passing of a legendary England career – and a clear choice for the all-time England dream team. Stanley Matthews had made his debut for England in 1934 and now a staggering 22 years and 228 days later he was playing for the 54th and last time for England at the remarkable age of forty-two.

1958 WORLD CUP QUALIFYING GROUP ONE FINAL TABLE

	P	W	D	L	GF	GA	P
England	4	3	1	0	15	5	7
Irish Rep	4	2	1	1	6	7	5
Denmark	4	0	0	4	4	13	0

Duncan Edwards, seen here in action against Scotland in 1957, was only twenty-two years old when he died in the Munich Air Crash. At that young age he had already accumulated 22 caps.

All four home countries qualified for the finals in Sweden – for the first and so far only time – which made the 1957/58 Home Championship, which immediately preceded the World Cup finals, more interesting than usual. England thrashed Wales 4-0 in Cardiff, then lost 3-2 to Northern Ireland at Wembley before beating the Scots 4-0 at Hampden Park.

The mid-season visitors to Wembley were France, another of the World Cup finalists. Despite the result against the Irish, Winterbottom now had a much-respected side, whose consistency was raising some eyebrows with Sweden just months away. Tommy Taylor and Bobby Robson, on his England debut, scored two each as England sent a message out to the other fifteen nations that they would be a force in Sweden. But the nation's expectations of World Cup success were soon to be dealt the unkindest and most unexpected blow of all.

On 6 February 1958, the flight carrying the Manchester United team home from a European Cup tie crashed on take-off at Munich airport killing eight people. Among those who died were the club's captain and England left-back Roger Byrne, who had been capped 33 times, centre forward Taylor, who had scored 7 times in his previous 10 England games (from a total of 16 goals in just 19 internationals) and the young Duncan Edwards. Considered by many to have been the best left half for a decade and an almost certain future England captain, Edwards had already been capped 18 times by England and had scored 5 goals. He survived the crash but died later in hospital.

England's first game after the tragedy was against the Scots in Glasgow and the side included one of the survivors of Munich as Bobby Charlton came into the England team for the first time. The young inside forward scored on his debut as England ran out 4-0 winners. The rising star of English football then scored both goals in the 2-0 defeat of Portugal. The England squad left for Sweden following a 5-0 defeat in Yugoslavia

Bobby Charlton, who scored on his England debut.

Yashin, the great Russian goalkeeper, punches away while being challenged by Johnny Haynes, World Cup finals 1958.

and a 1-1 draw in Moscow. All in all, there was little of the expectancy displayed just a few months before.

England's first game of the finals was against the USSR in Gothenburg. In a group including Brazil and Austria, England's task to qualify for the knock-out phase was not an easy one. Brazil were the clear favourites for the title and the Soviets were seen as one of the few sides that could halt the South Americans' progress. The England selectors picked the following side for the opening game:

McDonald (Burnley), Howe (West Bromwich Albion), Banks (Bolton Wanderers),

Clamp (Wolverhampton Wanderers), Wright (Wolverhampton Wanderers), Slater (Wolverhampton Wanderers), Douglas (Blackburn Rovers), Robson (West Bromwich Albion), Kevan (West Bromwich Albion), Haynes (Fulham), Finney (Preston North End).

The Soviets proved to be a more fluid, inventive and attractive side than England and it took them just thirteen minutes to score when Colin McDonald, who was to have a very good game, could only block a shot from Ilyin, allowing Simonian, who was following up, to score. They failed to increase their lead before the break but the second half was just ten minutes old when

England went 2-0 down. However, England did not give up the ghost and Wright brought his side back into the game with a looping free kick that the imposing Derek Kevan headed past the legendary Lev Yashin. England pressed for an equalizer and in the closing stages of the game it was Finney, who had carried on bravely after taking an early knock, who now led the comeback. With just six minutes remaining, Douglas was tripped in the box and Finney levelled the scores from the spot kick to secure England a hard-fought point.

All eyes were now fixed on England's selectors. The team had looked second best against the USSR and now faced mighty Brazil. The press saw Charlton as England's trump card, but he was not picked. Finney failed to recover from his injury and his replacement was to be Alan A'Court, who had played just once before for his country. England did, however, change their tactics for the game against Brazil using the strength of Don Howe in midfield alongside captain Wright. Luck also played a part to help England as Brazil left out Pele and Garrincha. However, they still played Didi; Bill Slater was given the role of shadowing him throughout the game.

Brazil dominated the first half. They hit the bar, had a shot cleared off the line and twice brought fine saves out of McDonald, but at the break had failed to convert superiority into goals. In the second half, England had more of the ball but, as the Brazilians had done in the first period, now England failed to make the most of their possession. Finney was sorely missed. England might even have had a penalty when Bellini pulled down Kevan. With neither team able to turn their advantage into goals, the game ended in

Zagallo, Brazil's winger, closes in on the English goalkeeper Colin McDonald during the 1958 World Cup match. The game ended 0-0.

a goalless draw – a very creditable result for England.

As the USSR had beaten Austria, the fourth side in the group, England now had to do the same to stay on course for a place in the quarter-finals. However, the same XI that had performed so well against the South Americans could only manage a 2-2 draw against the Austrians. England had failed to secure an automatic place in the knock-out stage and now waited on the result of the Brazil v. USSR game to discover their fate.

Brazil restored Pele and Garrincha to their side to face the Soviets. They won 2-0, a scoreline that severely flattered the Europeans who should have been beaten by a hatful. As goal difference did not count, England and the USSR were forced to play-off for a place in the next round. England brought in two new caps for the game, Peter Brabook, the Chelsea right-winger, and the

Wolves inside-right Peter Broadbent. To the surprise of the press, Haynes, who had failed to make an impact in the tournament so far, was still preferred to Charlton. As in the first game between the two, the Soviets dominated. England put up a spirited fight. Brabook hit the post twice, but the 1-0 defeat was a fair result and England were knocked out.

1958 WORLD CUP POOL FOUR FINAL TABLE

	P	W	D	L	GF	GA	P
Brazil	3	2	1	0	5	0	5
England	3	0	3	0	4	4	3
USSR	3	1	1	1	4	4	3
Austria	3	0	1	2	2	7	1

Play-off: USSR 1 England 0

England returned from a third World Cup campaign frustrated but, following the horror of Munich, little more could surely have been expected from Winterbottom's side. Meanwhile, Brazil marched on. A goal from Pele beat Wales, then the Brazilian number ten hit a hat-trick in the 5-2 win over France in the semi-finals before getting another two in another 5-2 win, in the final against the hosts, Sweden.

England's second game after the World Cup, following a thrilling 3-3 draw in Belfast, was at Wembley against the USSR. This was now the fourth meeting between the two countries in as many months. England were determined to avenge their defeat in Gothenburg and did so in no uncertain terms. Haynes found his form in an England shirt, hitting his only international hat-trick. Charlton and Lofthouse were restored to the side and both made their mark on the game with

a goal apiece as a more well-balanced England side than that which had appeared in the World Cup tore the Soviets apart 5-0.

England's game against the Scots at Wembley on 11 April 1959 was an unremarkable 1-0 victory made historic by the selection of Billy Wright. It was his 100th cap for England and on that day he became the first player from any country to achieve that milestone.

England toured South America in May 1959. Beforehand, Italy had visited Wembley and left with a 2-2 draw, both their goals being scored while England's Ron Flowers was off the pitch receiving treatment. The tour was a disaster for England as yet again South American opposition on their own soil proved too good for the English. The trip began with a defeat against Brazil in the Maracana stadium in front of a crowd of around 150,000 – the largest official attendance at any England game. This defeat was followed by defeats in Peru and then Mexico. A fourth game, against the USA in Los Angeles, saw England romp home 8-1 winners, with Charlton hitting three. This game also marked Wright's retirement from international football having amassed 105 caps since his debut in 1947. Remarkably, the USA game was his 70th consecutive England appearance and his 90th as captain. Unsurprisingly, Wright appears in England's all-time dream team.

The 1960/61 season was a good one for England. It began with a 5-2 win over Northern Ireland and continued with a 9-0 thrashing of Luxembourg, which included hat-tricks for both Jimmy Greaves and Charlton, a 4-2 win over Spain – di Stefano and all – and a 5-1 win over Wales. The England side going into the match with Scotland at Wembley in April 1961 was full

Billy Wright leads the team out against Scotland in April 1959 – and in doing so becomes the first England player to be awarded 100 caps. Originally playing in the right-half position, he latterly moved to centre half and used his jumping ability to overcome the accepted wisdom that a player needed to be 6ft plus to play in a central defensive role.

of confidence and looking forward to taking the Home Championship title and, more importantly, continue a run that had seen England remain undefeated against the Scots for a decade. Winterbottom's side picked itself:

R. Springett (Sheffield Wednesday), Armfield (Blackpool), McNeil (Middlesbrough), Robson (West Bromwich Albion), Swan (Sheffield Wednesday), Flowers (Wolverhampton Wanderers), Douglas (Blackburn Rovers), Greaves (Tottenham Hotspur), Smith (Tottenham Hotspur), Haynes (Fulham), Charlton (Manchester United).

It was a well-balanced team with a sprinkling of players who could be relied on to add flair to the proceedings while strength in the tackle was the prerequisite at the back. Playing in a 4-2-4 formation in front of Ron Springett, who had not

The England team that earned a 1-1 draw at Hampden Park in April 1960. From left to right, back row: Armfield, Slater, Flowers, Springett, Parry, Wilson. Front row: Connelly, Broadbent, Clayton, Baker, Charlton.

been fully tested in his eight previous internationals, were a world-class full-back in Jimmy Armfield and the sturdy, reliable Flowers. Haynes and Robson were a midfield pairing which any international manager would have envied. England had finally come across replacements, if such a thing was possible, for Matthews and Lofthouse in Douglas and Smith. Add to these the growing powers of Charlton plus the speed and ball skills of Greaves, only twenty years old but already the scorer of 11 goals in as many games for his country, and England's confidence was clearly not misplaced.

England broke open the Scots' defence after just nine minutes with a goal from Robson. Greaves then stepped forward and struck twice in nine minutes to extend England's lead to 3-0 with half an hour gone. The Scots, deciding that attack was the best form of defence, came back into the match early in the second half, struck twice, and looked capable of pulling the game out of the fire before their revival was punctured with a fourth goal from Douglas. England then stepped up a gear and in the final twenty minutes of the game overran the Scots with a performance of

Following England's 9-3 defeat of Scotland at Wembley in 1961, Johnny Haynes, the skipper, is hoisted shoulder high to celebrate the win. The other people in the picture are, from left to right: Flowers, Greaves, Swan, Armfield, McNeil, Winterbottom (in the background).

The England team that reached the quarter-finals of the 1962 World Cup. From left to right: Armfield, Moore, Norman, Springett, Flowers, Wilson. Front row: Greaves, Douglas, Hitchens, Haynes, R. Charlton.

breathtaking efficiency. Their fifth goal came after 73 minutes from Smith. Captain Haynes then scored twice in two minutes and Greaves completed his second international hat-trick with England's eighth goal. Shortly after, Smith added the ninth and the England side, denied a double figure score only by the final whistle, wallowed in an historic 9-3 win. It was the highest scoring game in the history of matches between the two countries. The twelve goals in the fixture also added to the record of 40 scored in the Home Championship that year.

1960/61 HOME CHAMPIONSHIP FINAL TABLE

	P	W	D	L	GF	GA	P
England	3	3	0	0	19	6	6
Wales	3	2	0	1	8	6	4
Scotland	3	1	0	2	8	13	2
N. Ireland	3	0	0	3	5	15	0

Winterbottom looked to the World Cup twelve months hence and, unsurprisingly, felt confident of his team's potential to make a determined assault on the title after three abortive attempts in the 1950s. However, a year would prove to be too long for this side. The 1961/62 Home Championship title went to Scotland, who won all their games, whereas England, with draws against Wales and Northern Ireland, finished in third place – their worst performance since the 1930s. Chile was awarded the 1962 World Cup but no one could see further than Brazil when it came to predicting the winners of the tournament.

England's opening group match, against Hungary, attracted fewer than 8,000 spectators but they were rewarded with two outstanding goals from the Hungarians who, at times, showed glimpses of the excellence of their famous predecessors. England looked second best throughout and although a Ron Flowers penalty

Action from the 1962 World Cup in Chile. Springett punches away from Bulgaria's Sokolov with Flowers and Wilson covering. The match ended scoreless.

minutes. A Charlton thunderbolt put England 2-0 up and then Greaves scored his side's third goal and his 20th in as many appearances. Argentina pulled one back but England's 3-1 win was well deserved and probably their best performance in the four World Cup finals they had qualified for up to and including 1962.

Hungary qualified with ease but England followed their fine performance against Argentina with a disappointing display against Bulgaria in what was widely regarded as the worst game of the tournament, the game ending in a 0-0 draw. However, England had qualified for the quarter-finals. An interesting aside to England's three games, all held at the Braden Copper Stadium, is the disappointing attendance figures. In total, just 23,432 people attended the three matches.

1962 WORLD CUP GROUP FOUR FINAL TABLE

	P	W	D	L	GF	GA	P
Hungary	3	2	1	0	8	2	5
England	3	1	1	1	4	3	3
Argentina	3	1	1	1	2	3	3
Bulgaria	3	0	1	2	1	7	1

England's opponents in the quarter-finals were red-hot favourites Brazil. England lined up as follows:

R. Springett (Sheffield Wednesday), Armfield (Blackpool), Wilson (Huddersfield Town), Moore (West Ham United), Norman (Tottenham Hotspur), Flowers (Wolverhampton Wanderers), Douglas (Blackburn Rovers), Greaves (Tottenham Hotspur), Hitchens (Inter Milan), Haynes (Fulham), Charlton (Manchester United).

levelled the scores at 1-1 on the hour the Magyars clinched their winner with fifteen minutes remaining.

Argentina had beaten Bulgaria in the other opening group match and now England needed to beat the South Americans to retain any hope of progressing in the competition. It was a tall order but Winterbottom brought in Alan Peacock, the Middlesbrough centre forward, for his international debut. The change reaped dividends as Peacock shone and England romped home to a 3-1 win after Flowers had given his side the platform for victory with a penalty after 17

England rose to the occasion and matched the illustrious South Americans in a memorable first half. Garrincha headed his side into a 1-0 lead but England responded well and Gerry Hitchens, the ex-Aston Villa centre forward, levelled the scores in what was to be the last of his 7 internationals, responding well to a Greaves header that had struck the bar. Garrincha turned on the style after the break and inspired his side to two goals in six minutes to bury England. First he drove in a powerful free kick which Springett could not hold and Vava slotted home, and then he chipped the England goalkeeper from 20 yards to make the final score 3-1. Outside of that six-minute spell England had matched the holders but it was the South Americans who marched on. After breezing past the hosts, Chile, in the semi-finals the Brazilians beat Czechoslovakia 3-1 in a one-sided final to take the Jules Rimet trophy for the second time.

On England's return, Winterbottom resigned the post of manager of the national team. He had been in the post since 1946 and was to make way for the first England player to become manager, Alf Ramsey. Winterbottom's last months in charge included the first leg of England's first foray into the European Nations Cup. The early rounds of the competition were two-leg knockout ties and England were drawn against France. The first leg, played at Hillsborough, ended in a disappointing 1-1 draw. Securing England's progress with an away win in Paris would be one of Ramsey's first tasks.

In Winterbottom's sixteen years as coach England's record flattered to deceive. They had played 139 games, won 78, drawn 33 and lost 28 – on the surface a creditable return. But in the key games, especially at the World Cup, England's

World Cup finals 1962. England lose 3-1 to Brazil and are out of the tournament. Here, the great Garrincha tangles with Ray Wilson.

performances were often below par. There can be little doubt that Winterbottom had laid the groundwork for what was to follow and that his achievements, particularly in the development of an established structure to the England set-up, were substantial. But perhaps his lack of experience in management before taking on the England job did hinder the progress of the side at the major tournaments.

The FA had earmarked Winterbottom's assistant, Jimmy Adamson, as the new England coach but he declined their offer. Their search then took them into club football and to East Anglia.

BILLY WRIGHT
Wolverhampton Wanderers
Half-back
105 international caps (1946-1959)

Captain of England on 90 occasions, Wright's longevity in the England shirt resulted from an inspired mid-career move from combative midfield player to central defender whilst playing in Switzerland during the 1954 World Cup Finals. Whilst not a tall man, his jumping ability was exceptional and that, coupled with his competitive spirit, enabled him to quickly master his new role. As a result he went on to earn his last 46 caps playing in the centre of defence and in so doing became the first footballer in the world to play over 100 times for his country.

TOM FINNEY
Preston North End
Wing/Centre forward
76 international caps (1946-1959)

Finney was one of the few top players who was clearly two footed and was happy playing in wide positions on either side of the pitch. He fulfilled both roles for England and also on occasions played at centre forward. His tally of 30 goals is excellent and he is remembered for the quality of many of his efforts. One of very few players to be selected for three World Cup squads, he was a truly world-class player. Following retirement from the game he was given a knighthood for his contribution to football.

BOBBY CHARLTON
Manchester United
Inside/Centre forward
106 international caps (1958-1970)

With Manchester United, Charlton was a winner of virtually every European club title from the Youth Cup through to the European Cup in 1968, when he captained the side. He topped all his many achievements when in 1966 he was a member of the successful World Cup team. He succeeded Billy Wright as the holder of the record number of caps for England, resulting from his international debut in 1958 aged twenty and his almost automatic selection for the next thirteen years. He scored 49 goals during 106 appearances and was European Footballer of the Year in 1966. A modest and unassuming person, he was honoured with a knighthood for services to football. The memories of his skill and dynamic shooting talent still remain with those privileged to have seen him play.

RAMON WILSON
Huddersfield Town/Everton
Left-back
63 international caps (1960-1968)

For nine years Wilson was a regular selection for England at full-back and it was under Alf Ramsey's management that most of his caps were awarded. Acknowledged as a competent defender he blossomed with Ramsey's 'wingless wonders' and became renowned for getting forward to support the attacking plays. He was England's most capped full-back at one time and a member of the 1966 World Cup-winning side.

CHAPTER**FOUR**

RAMSEY DELIVERS 1962-1966

Alf Ramsey was appointed England team manager in January 1963, following great success at Ipswich Town where he managed the side through three divisions and to a First Division title win in 1961/62.

Alf Ramsey was appointed manager of the England football team on 3 December 1962. Unlike his predecessor, Ramsey demanded complete control of team affairs. With that responsibility went a challenge that Winterbottom had not faced, namely the brickbats if the team failed. The new England manager had come late to the game, having begun his playing career with Southampton in 1946 after a spell as an amateur with Portsmouth. He became a regular in the Saints side the following season and in December 1948 won his first cap, against Switzerland.

Ramsey moved to another Second Division club, Tottenham, who won promotion in his first season at White Hart Lane, and he was back in an England shirt with the ill-starred 1950 World Cup side. He won his last England cap on the day the Hungarians came to Wembley and won 6-3. He had played 32 times for his country and scored 3 goals.

Ramsey entered management in 1955 with a Third Division side, Ipswich Town. Ramsey took the club into the Second Division in 1957 and, with little more than an average squad, he won the Second Division title in 1960/61 and then, remarkably, the First Division title the following year. He dispensed with an out-and-out winger and played an extra man behind the front three, ingraining a work ethic into his side that made them more than a match for more illustrious opponents. This largely unqualified run of managerial success meant his appointment as England manager was widely heralded.

But the new England manager faced a problem. If the England side were to play a 4-2-4 system, which suited the likes of Brazil, it would require some of his best players to play out of position. There was also a dearth of international-class wingers in the Football League. Instead of trying to forge international-class wingers out of inside forwards, Ramsey decided to do without them. So, he revised the 4-2-4 to a 4-3-3 system, which he felt suited the undoubted qualities of the English player: strength, fitness and morale.

Ramsey's first game as England manager was the second leg of the first-round European Nations Cup tie against France. The tournament prior to the semi-finals was staged on a home and away knock-out basis. The sides had drawn 1-1 at Hillsborough and now Ramsey looked optimistically for a win in Paris to progress to the second round of the competition. His first England team selection lined up as follows:

R. Springett (Sheffield Wednesday), Armfield (Blackpool), Henry (Tottenham Hotspur), Moore (West Ham United), Labone (Everton), Flowers (Wolverhampton Wanderers), Connelly (Burnley), Tambling (Chelsea), R. Smith (Tottenham Hotspur), Greaves (Tottenham Hotspur), R. Charlton (Manchester United).

All did not go to plan: Ron Springett had a nightmare game and England went out of the competition having been convincingly beaten 5-2. At least England were beaten by one of Europe's top sides – Holland were beaten over two legs by Luxembourg! In the final, Spain beat the USSR 2-1 to take the trophy.

April 1963 saw the Leicester City goalkeeper, Gordon Banks, come into the side for his debut in England's next match, at Wembley against the Scots. England lost this game too, then drew 1-1 at home to Brazil. It was hardly a glorious start for Ramsey.

After the Brazil match, England went off on a European summer tour. They started with a much-needed win, beating Czechoslovakia 4-2 with two goals from Greaves and one each from Bobby Smith and Charlton. The tour progressed to East Germany, where England won 2-1, and finished in Switzerland, where Charlton hit his third England hat-trick in a thumping 8-1 win. Ramsey was finally on his way.

Ramsey's first match as manager ended in a 5-2 defeat in Paris – a result that marked England's exit from the European Nations Cup.

The first game of the 1963/64 season brought an easy 4-0 win in Cardiff before a Rest of the World side, which included Yashin of Russia, Santos of Brazil, di Stefano of Spain, Seeler of West Germany and Puskas of Hungary, was entertained at Wembley. England won the game 2-1. In November 1963, England beat Northern Ireland 8-3 in the first Wembley international to be played under floodlights. Terry Paine of Southampton, playing wide on the right, scored a hat-trick while the irrepressible Greaves netted four. However, Ramsey knew that while beating the Irish at Wembley was one thing, winning the

England *v.* Brazil at Wembley in 1963 and England's Bobby Smith closes in on 'keeper Gylmar during the 1-1 draw.

World Cup for England in front of a somewhat sceptical home audience was very much another.

England's preparations for the finals began in earnest in the summer of 1964 with seven games in one month. Uruguay, Portugal and the Republic of Ireland were defeated before Ramsey's men departed for a tour of America. After trouncing the USA 10-0 in New York, Ramsey and his squad moved on to the less-than-happy hunting grounds of South America, where, like most European sides, England were given a salutary lesson on where the power lay in world football. The world champions, Brazil, were the ultimate test.

Pele was allowed the freedom of the park and orchestrated the game, the result of which was decided long before the final whistle. England took a 5-1 drubbing, the second time one of Ramsey's side had conceded as many goals. The next game, against Portugal in Sao Paulo, ended in a 1-1 draw and then England lost to Argentina 1-0 in Rio. Ramsey returned from Brazil with plenty to think about.

The 1964/65 season began with a hard-fought 4-3 win in Belfast and ended brightly for Ramsey as England won the Home Championship outright for the first time in five years.

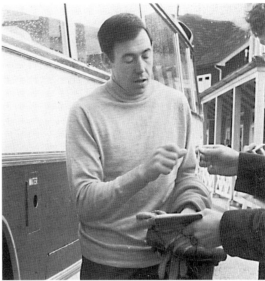

above: Gordon Banks made his debut in Ramsey's next selection and quickly established himself alongside Yashin of Russia as one of the two premier goalkeepers in Europe.

left: As Ramsey introduced new players and systems, the formation of his desired team began to emerge. Jimmy Greaves was clearly part of that process. As one of the most prolific goalscorers of his time he played regularly for the national side from 1957 until 1967, winning 57 caps and scoring 44 goals.

1964/65 HOME CHAMPIONSHIP FINAL TABLE

	P	W	D	L	GF	GA	P
England	3	2	1	0	8	6	5
Wales	3	2	0	1	9	4	4
Scotland	3	1	1	1	7	7	3
N. Ireland	3	0	0	3	5	12	0

A programme of four games in the summer of 1965 against European sides followed. Greaves got the only goal of the game against Hungary as Ramsey breathed a huge sigh of relief at a rare England clean-sheet. Two wins on the Continent was a very satisfactory return for Ramsey: 1-1 against Yugoslavia, 1-0 against West Germany and 2-1 against Sweden. The tour provided a platform for England's assault on the Jules Rimet trophy as the 1965/66 domestic season got underway.

However, Ramsey could still not find the strike force he wanted. A 0-0 draw against Wales in Cardiff was followed by a surprise home defeat at the hands of Austria. Terry Paine, Greaves and Barry Bridges were dropped for the visit of Northern Ireland. Bobby Charlton had emerged as an ever-present in the forward line, while his brother Jackie was making the centre-half role his own – but who to play alongside Bobby was Ramsey's biggest headache. He tried Alan Peacock

In the build-up to the 1966 World Cup, England met Hungary at Wembley, winning 1-0. In this photograph, Paine is trying to get a second goal for England but is foiled by the Hungarian 'keeper, Gelei.

of Leeds, Peter Thompson of Liverpool and Joe Baker of Arsenal. Peacock and Baker scored in the 2-1 win over Northern Ireland but Ramsey was the first to admit that he himself was still no nearer finding his most potent solution.

A possible turning point for Ramsey's selection conundrum came in December 1965, just six months before the finals were to begin. England visited Madrid and Ramsey lined up his side in a 4-3-3 formation. Out went the Manchester United winger John Connelly and in came the young Alan Ball:

Banks (Leicester City), Cohen (Fulham), Wilson (Huddersfield Town), Stiles (Manchester United), J. Charlton (Leeds United), Moore (West Ham United), Ball (Everton), Hunt (Liverpool), Baker (Arsenal), Eastham (Arsenal), R. Charlton (Manchester United).

above: England's squad for the 1966 World Cup. From left to right, back row: Shepherdson (trainer), Croker (assistant trainer), Hunt, Flowers, Bonetti, Springett, Banks, Moore, Greaves, Ramsey (manager). Middle row: Armfield, Callaghan, Byrne, Eastham, Hurst, J. Charlton, Ball, Stiles. Front row: Hunter, Cohen, Paine, Wilson, R. Charlton, Peters, Connelly.

below: England's opening game, against Uruguay, had the visitors defending for most of the match. Here, Jack Charlton tries hard to break the deadlock but goalkeeper Mazurkieviez intercepts.

The system worked a treat. England won 2-0 with goals from Roger Hunt and Baker. The Home Championship title was then won following a thrilling 4-3 victory over the Scots at Hampden Park with the West Ham centre forward Geoff Hurst getting his first England goal in this, his second game. The domestic season now over, five friendlies remained to be played in four weeks before the real action was to begin. England won them all, beating Yugoslavia, Finland, Norway, Denmark and Poland –

Bobby Charlton gets a header in that goes inches wide of the Mexican goal during England's second qualifying match, which they won 2-0.

none of which were among the sixteen nations who were preparing for the finals.

The curtain-raiser to the 1966 World Cup finals saw England take on Uruguay in a Group One match at Wembley. The visitors came to defend and England froze, unable to find a way through a solid South American defence. The result was a dreary 0-0 draw. England's main rivals for the title fared better. Brazil beat Bulgaria 2-0 at Goodison Park with two stunning free kicks from Pele and Garrincha. The Portuguese team were flattered by the 3-1 defeat of Hungary at Old Trafford, while the West Germans breezed comfortably past the Swiss, 5-0. The first shock of the tournament came in the second set of games when Brazil, without Pele, were beaten 3-1 by Hungary in one of the classic games of World Cup history.

England's second game was against Mexico, who played even more defensively than had the Uruguayans. It took England almost until half-time to break down the Mexican defence, Bobby Charlton hitting a scorching right-footed drive from outside the penalty area past Calderon to give England the lead. Although Hunt added a second, following good work from Bobby Charlton and Greaves, it was an unconvincing performance from Ramsey's side. His attackers – Paine, Greaves, Charlton, Hunt and Peters – were still not functioning as a potent unit.

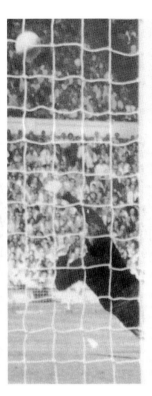

Geoff Hurst (on ground) sees his goal attempt punched away by Argentine goalkeeper Roma during the World Cup semi-final as Charlton and Ball look on anxiously.

With two of four teams progressing from each of the four groups to the knock-out phase, the first hurdle had been crossed. But Ramsey wanted to stay playing at Wembley, so England would have to beat the French in their final group match to make sure of keeping what was perceived to be a huge psychological advantage.

Uruguay had beaten the French and, with two goals from Hunt, so did England. However, it had not been an inspirational performance. Ramsey had used Liverpool's Ian Callaghan as an orthodox winger but, without Ball stoking the engine room, England's threat was diminished. Ramsey decided that the wingers should go and

the midfield would have to work harder. Another spanner was thrown into the works as Greaves picked up an injury. The fans' favourite and England's most prolific striker now looked doubtful for the next game as the 1966 World Cup moved into its sudden-death phase.

1966 WORLD CUP GROUP ONE FINAL TABLE

	P	W	D	L	GF	GA	P
England	3	2	1	0	4	0	5
Uruguay	3	1	2	0	2	1	4
Mexico	3	0	2	1	1	3	2
France	3	0	1	2	2	5	1

Thus far unconvincing but defensively secure (Banks had yet to be beaten), England now faced the Argentines in the quarter-finals, for whom 'brilliant yet temperamental' was proving to be a fair assessment. On the day, the teams would be involved in one of the most controversial matches in World Cup history. Ramsey left out a questionably fit Greaves in favour of Hurst, for his first game of the tournament, while Ball was recalled in place of Callaghan as England adopted a wingless formation.

England soon experienced the cynical side of the South Americans' approach as flying tackles went in every time England threatened the Argentine goal in the first quarter of the game. Herr Kreitlein, the German referee, tried courageously to keep on top of the game as it threatened to get out of hand. Every time he blew his whistle, the Argentine captain, Rattin, would be at his heels. Soon he was booked, for a foul on Bobby Charlton. This failed to subdue the Argentine and, with just nine minutes of the first half remaining, he was sent off after complaining about another booking for one of his team-mates. Rattin refused to go. The referee remained unmoved as FIFA officials stepped into the fray and then, with a major confrontation looking likely, even the police intervened. Suddenly it appeared as though the Argentine manager was beckoning his side from the pitch. The England players sat and watched. Eventually, fully ten minutes after his dismissal, Rattin left and the game restarted.

As so often happens when a team loses a player, the ten began to outplay the eleven. Despite this, Argentina could not break through the England defence and the few clear-cut

Rattin, the Argentina captain, protests once too often and is ordered off. After ten minutes of argument he eventually departed.

chances in the game fell to the home side. Just after the break, Hurst brought a wondrous save from Roma and, as the ten started to tire, England began to impose as the threat of Onega, through whom all Argentina's creative play had seemed to flow, diminished.

The game entered its last quarter hour and looked bound for extra time until Martin Peters looped a high cross into the Argentine area and his West Ham team-mate Hurst headed England into a winning lead. At the final whistle there was no jubilation at the victory, only a feeling of relief in the England camp at a hurdle cleared.

The Argentines did not take their defeat well. Stories abounded of threatening behaviour by the South Americans, aimed at England players and the match officials, in the tunnel after the game and of vandalism of their Wembley dressing room. The England manager had famously stopped his players exchanging shirts with their opponents at the end of the match and Ramsey's response after the game was 'Our best football will come against the team which comes out to play football, and not to act as animals!' The England manager's actions and outburst were to be remembered longer in some quarters of world football than the behaviour that had prompted them.

The 1966 World Cup thus far had made many of the wrong headlines. England had been uninspiring. Pele had been kicked out of the World Cup by two Portuguese defenders, Vicente and Morais. Uruguay, Argentina and West Germany had won few friends. Now, on the eve of the semi-finals a new controversy blew up. Portugal's Eusebio, the tournament's top scorer, expressed his anxiety that Nobby Stiles, who had attracted the gaze of a few Ramsey detractors with his no-nonsense approach, might prefer to stifle his undoubted talents by foul means as well as fair. This outburst put a great deal of pressure on Ramsey as Stiles was such an integral part of his team. Although there was substantial pressure on the manager to rest the Manchester United number four, Ramsey stuck by his player, refusing to change a winning side. More than any other player, Stiles would be under the spotlight as the day of the semi-final approached.

It was a warm July evening and the tension inside Wembley was greater than for any of England's previous games. There was still no place in the England line-up for Greaves as Ramsey announced an unchanged side from that which had defeated Argentina. The game began quietly and, to the relief of everyone, without any of the incidents that had marred two of the four-quarter finals: the contest was almost half an hour old before the French referee blew his whistle for a foul. It was England who dominated the early skirmishes and should have taken a grip where it mattered most, but over-eagerness saw three good chances fall to Hurst and all three spurned. It seemed to many in the 94,000 crowd that this time England would sorely miss their poacher supreme, Greaves.

However, after half an hour, Wilson, who had been one of the undoubted stars of England's side to date, found Hunt on the edge of the Portuguese penalty area. The England striker's shot cannoned onto the legs of the Portuguese goalkeeper, Jose Pereira, and rebounded to Bobby Charlton who calmly drove the ball home: 1-0 to England.

Eusebio took up the challenge thrown down by England and before the break struck a shot which Banks could not hold. Stiles cleared the danger only for the Portuguese star to turn the England defence inside out on a jinking run. After half-time the red-shirted Portuguese, using quick, incisive passing movements which made it look as though they had more than a dozen men on the pitch, had England's midfield on the rack. As the minutes ticked slowly by, England looked increasingly desperate for that two-goal cushion which would be too much for their opponents. It came with just eleven minutes remaining.

The move began with England's captain, Bobby Moore, who sent George Cohen down the right

An incident in one of the great games of the 1966 World Cup: Eusebio, the Portuguese star of the tournament, challenges the ever-competitive Nobby Stiles.

The Charlton brothers, relaxed and happy to be in the World Cup final.

wing with a raking pass. Cohen kept the momentum going by finding Hurst. As the noise of the 94,000 spectators built to a crescendo, Hurst shrugged off two challenges and spotted Bobby Charlton moving into a threatening position. He laid the ball off to the England number nine who drove his shot low and true. Like the top being blasted from a volcano, Wembley erupted. The scoreboard ticked over: England 2 Portugal 0. Jose Augusta, the Portuguese midfielder, reached out his hand to Charlton – he felt his team was beaten.

Portugal had apparently given their all but now they got a piece of the luck which so far had deserted them as Banks misjudged a cross, Torres headed for goal and Jack Charlton stopped the ball crossing the line with his arm. Eusebio converted the penalty but his side could give no more. At the final whistle England's players were overcome with emotion, while the Portuguese stood around, dazed at their defeat.

Alf Ramsey's pre-tournament promise of World Cup triumph for England had rung around the country. Some believed him, most did not. But England had now reached the final, through hard graft, a little luck and the 'Ramsey factor'. Now the day of reckoning dawned. Would Ramsey deliver his promise or would England fall to the Germans, who had beaten the USSR 2-1 in a dour match at Goodison Park in the other semi-final?

World Cup fever gripped the nation in those four days between semi-final and final. There was now no call to restore Greaves and Ramsey grasped at the luxury of announcing another unchanged side. The Germans made one change, with Hottges coming into the team in place of Lutz at right-back. Having been presented to the Queen, the two adversaries lined up for the kick-off as follows:

The teams and officials await the kick-off.

England: Banks (Leicester City), Cohen (Fulham), Wilson (Everton), Stiles (Manchester United), J. Charlton (Leeds United), Moore (West Ham United), Ball (Blackpool), Hunt (Liverpool), R. Charlton (Manchester United), Hurst (West Ham United), Peters (West Ham United).

West Germany: Tilkowski (Borussia Dortmund), Hottges (Werder Bremen), Schulz (Hamburg), Weber (Cologne), Schnellinger (Milan), Haller (Bologna), Beckenbauer (Bayern Munich), Overath (Cologne), Seeler (Hamburg), Held (Borussia Dortmund), Emmerich (Borussia Dortmund).

Helmut Schon, the German manager, labelled Bobby Charlton as the England danger-man. The England number nine had played an inspired game in the semi-final and Schon gave the young Franz Beckenbauer the task of extinguishing the Charlton influence. Ramsey, meanwhile, saw Beckenbauer as the German's possible match-winner and the sight of the young number seven chasing after Charlton instead of imposing himself on the game gave the England manager an early boost. A downpour of rain made for a slippery surface but both teams settled quickly. England found the back of their opponents' net first as Hurst collided with Tilkowski. The ball fell to Moore who slotted it into the German net only to see his 'goal' disallowed.

Undeterred, England kept up the early pressure, as Martin Peters brought an acrobatic save out of Tilkowski with a shot from 20 yards, and then from a similar distance drove a second just two feet wide. As early as the tenth minute it was clear that the game had the makings of an open, exciting contest – something which the Wembley crowd at England's previous games had seen little of. England's defence had conceded just two goals in its previous ten games but, after 13 minutes, a cross

above: Returning after half time, one goal apiece and all to play for.

left: Alan Ball, the dynamo of the England team, is quick to offer some early advice to the Swiss referee, Gottfried Dienst, while Bobby Charlton and George Cohen also have a say.

from Held was met by Wilson. Instead of heading clear, he headed straight to Haller, who steadied himself, twisted round and drove past a despairing Banks to put his side a goal to the good. The Germans sat back on their early lead, allowing Ramsey's side to respond with an equalizer within six minutes. Moore was brought down for a free kick and, catching the German defence offguard, quickly hit a 35-yard ball into the German box which, having timed his run to perfection, freed Hurst from his marker to head low past the German goalkeeper to level the scores at 1-1.

Invigorated by the goal, Moore and Bobby Charlton began to shine. Indeed, had Charlton been on the receiving end of some of his own crosses England might have gone in at half time on top. However, at the break the teams were level at 1-1, with the Germans also scenting victory as England were indebted to Banks for two point-blank saves, from Emmerich and Overath.

After the breathless start to the first half, it was almost a relief as the second began more quietly – it was as if the players now realized that they were in for a long day. Few chances were created over the next 30 minutes. Bobby Charlton had a dubious penalty appeal turned down, but then with just 15 minutes left to play Hunt found the outstanding Ball, whose shot Tilkowski could not hold and a corner was conceded. From it, Hottges blocked a shot from Hurst but the alert Peters grasped the chance to half-volley the ball from five yards into the German net. That would surely be enough – England's solid back line would see them through. So it seemed as Lady Luck smiled on the team in red when Weber missed a golden chance to level the scores with just a couple of minutes remaining.

The game entered its 90th minute and the Germans threw everything forward for a last-gasp attack. They won a free kick in a dangerous position

above: Overath kicks the ball out for a corner under pressure from Peters, Hunt, Hurst and Cohen.

right: Alan Ball's performance in the final was outstanding: he competed for every ball and was still running after two hours of play. This shot shows him bursting through between the West German 'keeper and a defender – typical of his play throughout the day.

after Jack Charlton was adjudged to have climbed over Seeler. Emmerich jabbed the ball forward into the crowded England penalty box. Schnellinger looked to have handled, a German goal-bound strike hit the back of one of their own players and in the mêlée the ball fell to Weber and the German defender slotted home to send the game into extra time. Barely had England restarted the game when the referee blew for full time: 2-2.

The German goal was a body blow but Ramsey responded as his players, in stunned disbelief, gathered round the manager taking in drinks and advice, the stadium now in silence. His manner was angry but unshaken and his message sure: 'You've won it once. You've proved you can win it. Now go out and win it again.' He may not have been Nelson or Churchill, but at that moment Ramsey seemed just as important a figure in the history of the nation. Both sets of players appeared sapped of their strength but Ramsey implored his

side for one more great effort, pointing out to his XI that the Germans looked spent.

To their credit England responded and grasped the initiative at the restart as the tireless Ball brought a wonderful save from Tilkowski with a 20-yard drive. The errors mounted, the pace slowed and the defensive gaps grew larger. Bobby Charlton hit another shot, which the German goalkeeper pushed against the post. The Germans responded by opening up the England defence but they now lacked the finishing touch to punish the home side.

The pendulum swung again midway through the first half of extra time. Stiles released Ball on the right, he centred and Hurst trapped the ball, turned, and in one move drove his shot hard onto the underside of the German bar. The ball bounced down and was cleared, but did it cross the line? The entire England team appealed, not unnaturally, for a goal. Referee Dienst ran across to his linesman, the Russian Tofik Bakhramov and for what seemed like an age the great stadium was silent. The man in black then turned on his heels and signalled to the centre circle – the goal was given and Wembley erupted. The Germans crowded the referee pleading with him to change his mind. He didn't and the fight was almost visibly seen to drain from them. The most controversial goal of any World Cup final? Of that there can be no doubt, but the Germans had been fortunate to take the game into extra time and now they did not look capable of a second comeback.

In the final minute of extra time, the England captain and the rock of his team's defence, made the last of many telling passes of an unblemished World Cup to find his club-mate Hurst on the halfway line. A last burst of energy saw the England number ten break past his marker and head towards the German goal. 'Some people are on the pitch. They think it's all over…' Hurst looked up and completed his hat-trick

The deciding moment of the third England goal. Was the ball fully over the line? Bobby Charlton thinks it is and so do the linesman and the referee.

above: The final whistle and Ramsey stays in his seat – he said England would win the World Cup and so they have.

left: Banks shows how the players felt when the whistle blew for full time.

with a cracking drive, which left Tilkowski rooted to the ground '...It is now!' said BBC TV commentator, Kenneth Wolstenhome, and with those words reserved his own place in English football history.

It was indeed all over. England had won 4-2, and within a few short moments Bobby Moore was leading his side up the thirty-nine steps to the Royal Box. Instinctively, Moore wiped his grubby hands on his shirt and shorts before taking the golden Jules Rimet trophy from the Queen. Moore and his side then began a glorious lap of honour, while a spontaneous chorus of God Save The Queen echoed round the stadium.

The England team lifted Moore, holding the World Cup raised in triumph, onto the shoulders of Cohen and Hurst, photographs of which were probably the most memorable of the entire afternoon. The scenes of the players celebrating their remarkable victory, such as Stiles dancing with the World Cup, are icons in the history of the game in England.

Away from Wembley, the nation rejoiced until long into the night. Trafalgar Square became the centre of impromptu celebrations in London while thousands gathered outside the Kensington Gardens Hotel where the victorious side were banqueting. They emerged, with the trophy and the

Bobby Moore receives the Jules Rimet World Cup trophy from Queen Elizabeth II.

Prime Minister, to the delight of the crowd before partying the night away.

The following day's *Sunday Times*, under the heading 'London goes mad after World Cup victory', reported thus on the celebrations in the capital:

London went mad last night after England's 4-2 victory in one of the most fantastic finals in the history of the World Cup. The celebrations culminated in a jubilant demonstration in Latin American style outside the hotel in Kensington High Street where a reception was being held for the players. Cars jammed all the way along the street took up the 'England England' beat on their horns. Inside the hotel, Mr Harold Wilson received the guests from FIFA, the FA, the English and West German teams, and players and representatives from the other fourteen countries who took part in the final stages of the 1966 World Cup. One highly honoured guest was Mr David Corbett, whose mongrel dog, Pickles,

Ray Wilson parades with the World Cup trophy – enjoying his moment of glory.

found the World Cup after it had been stolen. Mr Corbett took the dog out to meet the delighted crowd.

When the England team appeared on a balcony, 100 policemen could hardly contain the crowd as they roared their approval when the gold Jules Rimet trophy was held aloft. Hundreds more England supporters danced and sang in Trafalgar Square. Blowing bugles, ringing bells and sounding horns, the supporters, led by a youth holding a replica of the World Cup,

pranced through the crowds singing 'We've got the whole world in our hands'.

The England win received mixed reports around the world. In Argentina, the *Cronica* called the final a 'farce' and *Ultima Hora* called England's side 'Lucky Pirates'. Others were more complimentary: the German newspaper *Nachtausgabe* called the game 'A Great Final' and Brazilian radio described England as being worthy winners. In Rome, *Il Messaggero's* headline was 'They win wars and cups'.

FOREVER
ENGLAND

right: The celebrations in the stadium went on and on: Moore holds the trophy aloft for the nation to see.

below: The victory parade goes on – hat-trick hero Geoff Hurst takes his turn to lead the celebrations.

England World Cup winners, 1966. From left to right, back row: Shepherdson (trainer), Stiles, Hunt, Banks, J. Charlton, Cohen, Wilson, Ramsey (manager). Front row: Peters, Hurst, Moore (captain), Ball, R. Charlton.

Ramsey was knighted in the 1967 New Year's honours list, while over time every member of the side also received honours from the Queen. Five of the eleven – Moore, Bobby Charlton, Banks and the defensive pairing of Cohen and Wilson – feature in England's hall of fame. What is perhaps most remarkable about England's win in 1966 is that over the years the nation's recall and

fondness of the team, the event, the goals and even the BBC's television commentary has strengthened rather than diminished. More than three decades after the game, the players are regularly quoted as saying that not a day goes by without someone wanting to talk to them about that great day in '66.

The strong bond between captain Bobby Moore and manager Alf Ramsey made a major contribution to England's fine performances during the 1960s.

BOBBY MOORE
West Ham United
Half-back/Midfield
108 international caps (1962-1973)

A natural leader who led by example, Moore was recognised worldwide as one of the great players of all time. Brilliant in the tackle and ice cool in any situation, he captained England to their World Cup triumph in 1966. By the time his international career ended in 1973 he had overtaken Bobby Charlton as the record cap holder and finished with 108 appearances, of which 90 were as captain. His West Ham club side won the European Cup Winners Cup in 1965 and he was also voted Footballer of the Year in 1964 and Player of the Tournament at the 1970 World Cup. The awards of first an OBE then a knighthood was a just recognition of his contribution to England's footballing history.

GORDON BANKS
Leicester City/Stoke City
Goalkeeper
73 international caps (1963-1972)

A world-class player in every aspect of the goalkeepers' trade, recognition came late to 'Banksy'. He was twenty-five before he got his first cap but he went on to total 73 over the ten years that he was England's number one – setting a record for a goalkeeper at that time. Footballer of the Year and Sportsman of the Year in 1972, he is always remembered for his amazing save from Pele in the 1970 World Cup in Mexico. The first 'keeper in international football to keep over 10 clean sheets, he was an inspiration to the 1966 World Cup-winning side. He sadly lost an eye in a road accident in 1973, but still made some appearances in American soccer after that – he did not like being beaten!

ALAN BALL
Blackpool/Everton/Arsenal
Forward/Midfield
72 international caps (1965-1975)

Another World Cup winner, on that World Cup final day in 1966 Alan Ball was special. Very special indeed, in fact! He outran every player on the field, chased every ball, competed for every half chance: his team were going to win and they did. This game was the highlight of his career, but it was also typical of every game he ever played. England's grafter in midfield, his hard work earned him 72 caps over eleven years. Never a big goalscorer, he only bagged 8, but if assists were counted he would be up there with anybody. As a mark of his quality as a player, in 1971 he became the subject of the British record transfer fee (£220,000) when he joined Arsenal from Everton.

GEOFF HURST
West Ham Utd
Forward/Striker
49 international caps (1966-1972)

This is a player who will be talked about for many years to come, having scored a hat-trick in England's 1966 World Cup final success – the only time it has been achieved. A traditional English centre forward, he could take the roughhouse of the penalty box without complaint. With good all-round ability, he also boasted an enviable strike rate – not many international forwards have a goal return rate of almost 50 per cent (24 goals in 49 games). An important player in West Ham's 1960s successes, he contributed to their FA Cup win and European exploits in 1965.

Moore and Peters can only watch as Dennis Law, Scotland's talented inside forward, strikes for goal in the old enemy's 3-2 win in April 1967.

England played just three games as world champions before the visit of the Scots. They first beat Northern Ireland and then Wales in Home Championship games, which were also doubling up as qualification matches for the 1968 European Nations Cup. Then they were held to a 0-0 draw by Czechoslovakia in a friendly match at Wembley. In all three games, Ramsey fielded his World Cup-winning XI.

For the visit of the Scots, Ramsey recalled Jimmy Greaves in place of Roger Hunt – which led the Scots to comment that England were now strengthening their side for the visit of Bobby Brown's Scotland team. Brown, newly installed as manager, had done his homework and selected a side that he felt would dominate the midfield and deprive England of the space and time which they would require to play their game. Ray Wilson was also selected for England, although not fully fit.

The Scots began the match brightly and, when Jack Charlton was badly injured in the eleventh minute, a shock result seemed possible. As a result of Charlton's injury, Martin Peters was forced into a defensive role and given the job of marking Dennis Law. This change, with no substitutions allowed, also meant that Geoff Hurst and Greaves were deprived of their main supply channel.

Scotland took full advantage of England's misfortune and took the lead through Law. They could, and should, have increased their advantage before the break, such was their domination of the game. However, they seemed to be more interested in embarrassing England by depriving their hosts of the ball than they were in scoring goals. Although England came back early in the second half with a number of half-chances, the Scots extended their lead with twelve minutes left as Lennox beat Gordon Banks with a rasping drive.

It was only then, when two goals adrift, that England finally got into the game and halved the deficit as the limping Jack Charlton scored. Almost immediately, Law brought a world-class save from Banks, who arched back to tip the Manchester United striker's lob over the bar. But a third Scotland goal soon came as McCalliog and Wallace combined for the former to bury the ball in the back of the England net. Hurst pulled another back to make the score 2-3, but it was in vain as England's nineteen-match unbeaten run came to an end against the one side they would least have liked to have lost it to. English red faces, yes, but this one result was the only major setback for England in terms of qualification for the quarter-finals of the European Nations Cup.

1968 EUROPEAN NATIONS CUP QUALIFYING GROUP EIGHT FINAL TABLE

	P	W	D	L	GF	GA	P
England	6	4	1	1	15	5	9
Scotland	6	3	2	1	10	8	8
Wales	6	1	2	3	6	12	4
N. Ireland	6	1	1	4	2	8	3

The first of the two quarter-final games against the Spanish was played at Wembley. Bobby Charlton scored the only goal of the game and then Ramsey's side completed their victory a month later with a 2-1 win in Madrid, thanks to goals from Peters and the Leeds midfielder, Norman Hunter, to register a very creditable 3-1 aggregate win.

The two semi-finals and the final of the tournament were held in Italy. England, as world champions, were not only favourites to win their semi-final against Yugoslavia but were expected to take the title as they were widely regarded as being superior to Italy and the USSR, the other semi-finalists. England lined up for their most

important game since the World Cup final as follows:

Banks (Stoke City), Newton (Blackburn Rovers), Wilson (Everton), Mullery (Tottenham Hotspur), Labone (Everton), Moore (West Ham United), Ball (Everton), Peters (West Ham United), R. Charlton (Manchester United), Hunt (Liverpool), Hunter (Leeds United).

All did not go to plan. England had lost a hard-fought encounter against West Germany in Hanover just days before and were clearly not fully recovered, whereas their opponents had rested in the build-up to the game. In an ill-tempered match, Alan Mullery became the first England player to be sent off in a full international. Down to ten men, England battled bravely and were just seconds from taking the game into extra time when Dzajic scored the

Alan Mullery was a fine competitive midfielder who has the unenviable record of being the first England player to be sent off. Despite this setback, he still earned 35 caps between 1964 and 1971.

Terry Neill, Northern Ireland's central defender, frustrates Alan Ball during an England attack. The match, played at Windsor Park in May 1969, was won 3-1 by England.

Jackie Charlton heads home the winning goal in the 1-0 win over Portugal in December 1969.

only goal of the game for Yugoslavia to take them through to the final.

The hosts, Italy, beat the Yugoslavs in a replayed final and England achieved some consolation by seeing off the USSR in an excellent third-place play-off match. Hurst was restored to the side and scored one of England's two goals in the 2-0 win, Bobby Charlton getting the other. After reaching the semi-final of the European Nations Cup for the first time, England ended the year with two uninspiring draws, against Romania and Bulgaria, to end 1968 on a disappointing note.

A whitewash of the three home nations, including a fine 4-1 win over the Scots at Wembley, saw England take the 1969 Home Championship title before embarking on a summer trip to Mexico, the venue for the forthcoming 1970 World Cup finals, for which England had already qualified as holders. England's acclimatization trip began in Mexico City, where Ramsey's team drew 0-0 with the national side, before progressing to Montevideo

where they beat the Uruguayans 2-1. Their final game, in Rio, ended in a 2-1 defeat at the hands of Brazil. Although the results were mixed, the England squad returned home with a greater understanding of the tough challenge that lay ahead if England were to retain the World Cup.

England played seven games during the 1969/70 season before the World Cup and were unbeaten in all of them. The run included creditable 1-0 wins against Holland and Portugal, while the game against Scotland ended in a goalless draw for the first time since 1872. England were finding goals hard to come by, although Ramsey's side were still proving very difficult to break down. As the squad departed for Mexico to the sound of their first record release, 'Back Home', which was sitting on top of the charts, the nation was cautiously optimistic about the team's chances.

England's preparations for the finals were completed at a camp in Colombia. While based there, England beat the national side 4-0 in

Bobby Moore bursts through the Welsh defence in the Home Championship match in Cardiff, April 1970.

Bogota and then beat Ecuador 2-0 in Quito. However, it was not the games that made the headlines but an incident that had the England captain on the front pages of newspapers around the world.

The squad was staying at the Tequendama Hotel in Bogota. During some free time, Bobby Moore and Bobby Charlton visited the Green Fire jewellery shop inside the hotel. A few minutes later, Moore was approached and accused of stealing a bracelet from the shop. He was held for four days, unable to travel back to Mexico with the rest of the squad, while the police investigated the incident. After diplomatic intervention by the British government, the England captain was released on bail and later the case was dropped. Two years later, in what resulted in a conspiracy case, the local perpetrators were tried. Now back to full strength, the incident only seemed to make England even more determined to bring the World Cup home.

The squad that represented England in the 1970 World Cup in Mexico. From left to right, back row: Oakes, Hunter, O'Grady, Hunt, Reaney, Newton, Bell, Wright, Banks, Peters, Moore, Hurst, Shepherdson. Front row: Lee, Cooper, Coates, Thompson, Mullery, J. Charlton.

The Mexico World Cup proved to be one of the best in the history of the competition. Brazil, with Jairzinho, Rivelino and the rejuvenated Pele, were clear favourites. England, West Germany, Uruguay and Italy were tipped as the teams who would play the supporting roles. The bookmakers had given England a fair chance of retaining their crown, while some commentators believed that Sir Alf's 1970 squad was better than the one which had won the World Cup four years before.

Whatever their potential, England were to be put to the sternest of tests as Brazil, Czechoslovakia and Romania were their opponents in the hardest of the four first-round groups. It was important for England to get off to a winning start against Romania. Ramsey's side, lining-up in a 4-4-2 formation, was booed onto the Jalisco Stadium pitch in Guadalajara by a partisan 50,000 crowd who wanted to see the holders, whom they saw as the epitome of negative football, fall at the first hurdle. The England side was:

Banks (Stoke City), Newton (Everton), Cooper (Leeds United), Mullery (Tottenham Hotspur), Labone (Everton), Moore (West Ham United), Lee (Manchester City), Ball (Everton), Charlton (Manchester United), Hurst (West Ham United), Peters (Tottenham Hotspur).

England took a physical buffeting from the Romanians, which went largely unchecked by the Belgian referee. It resulted in Keith Newton having

above: Moore and Peters, England and West Ham team-mates, relax at an England training session.

right: An incident from England's first match in the 1970 World Cup in Mexico. Hurst rises to challenge Romanian goalkeeper Sterica but fails to connect. Hurst had more success later, scoring the goal in the 1-0 victory.

to go off after 50 minutes, with the game still delicately poised at 0-0, only for the same player to dole out similar treatment to his replacement, Everton's Tommy Wright. Ramsey needed a win. He sent on Chelsea's Peter Osgood for Francis Lee, but it was Hurst who broke the deadlock after 65 minutes with a goal to which the Romanians had no reply. Although uninspiring, England had begun their defence of the title with a win.

The next fixture, England v. Brazil, was the most eagerly awaited game of all the group matches in Mexico. It did not disappoint. It was the clash of the titans, the winners in 1958 and 1962 against the winners in 1966. In the baking afternoon heat at Guadalajara, the Brazilians were favourites but

were caught off guard by a resolute England side who dominated the early stages of the game. However, England's superiority did not result in goals. Brazil regrouped and began to come back into the game. In one never-to-be-forgotten incident, Carlos Alberto released Jairzinho down the right flank, he crossed from the dead-ball line and Pele soared above the England defence to head low and hard to the foot of Banks's right-hand post – a certain goal. Banks pounced along his goal line and, as the ball bounced inches in front of him, he flicked it up and over the bar. It was a wondrous save and possibly the most talked about in the history of the World Cup.

But Brazil were not to be denied and had better luck after 59 minutes when Pele, threatening

inside the England penalty box, sensed his winger Jairzinho pounding down the right. He laid off a perfect ball which his team-mate drove past Banks to break the deadlock.

In response, Ramsey brought on Jeff Astle for Lee and Colin Bell for Charlton, a move that gave life to England's chances of getting back into the game. Astle set up Alan Ball only to see him miskick a good opening, and then the West Bromwich Albion centre forward found himself clear with the ball at his feet in front of the

The Brazilians are upset over Lee's challenge on goalkeeper Felix and England's number seven gets a booking.

Brazil's Santana closes in on Bobby Charlton during their World Cup match in 1970.

Brazilian goal. It was England's best chance of the match but his shot, on his weaker left foot, ran tamely across the goal and wide of the left-hand upright. Ball subsequently hit the post but England were ultimately beaten 1-0. It had been a classic game between two great sides.

The second half had also witnessed one of the most remembered moments in England's history. It was not a goal, not a save, not a sending-off but a tackle, by Moore, who effortlessly stole the ball from Jairzinho inside the England box and in a single move turned to bring the ball out of defence in a memorable piece of individual brilliance. At the end of the game, Moore and Pele, two of the world's greatest-ever players, embraced and swapped shirts. The long-standing mutual admiration between the two men and their two sides was genuine and while the match confirmed Brazil as hot favourites it also supported England's claim to be the best Europe had to offer.

Brazil made heavy weather of Romania, beating them 3-2, while a day later England faced up to the least accomplished of the sides in their group, Czechoslovakia. England needed only a draw to progress in the tournament.

Ramsey recalled Jack Charlton to the heart of his defence and gave a debut to Charlton's Leeds United club-mate, Allan Clarke. The game, which marked Bobby Charlton's equalling of Billy Wright's 105 caps for England, never looked like reaching the heights of the Brazil game and a dubious penalty for England, successfully converted by Clarke, provided England with a win and qualification for the quarter-finals.

The famous shirt exchange between Pele and Moore. There were many occasions on which these two fine players met and from those confrontations developed a mutual respect, the true feeling of which is shown in this photograph.

1970 WORLD CUP
GROUP THREE FINAL TABLE

	P	W	D	L	GF	GA	P
Brazil	3	3	0	0	8	3	6
England	3	2	0	1	2	1	4
Romania	3	1	0	2	4	5	2
Czech	3	0	0	3	2	7	0

above: The game against Czechoslovakia was a special occasion for Bobby Charlton as he made his 105th appearance for his country, equalling Billy Wright's record.

left: A young Allan Clark made his debut in the last 1970 qualifying match in England's group when the side defeated Czechoslovakia 1-0 (through a penalty which Clarke converted).

England now faced West Germany. The Germans had come through the easiest group of the first phase, scoring 10 goals in their 3 matches, 7 of them from rising star Gerd Muller. The rerun of the 1966 final was the pick of the round but for England, and Ramsey, it was to mark a downturn in fortunes. The writing was on the wall for Ramsey as the world's number one goalkeeper, Gordon Banks, had to pull out of the team after being taken ill on the morning of the match. It was a particular blow for the player, who had been awarded his OBE just days before the encounter. Ramsey called on Banks' deputy, Chelsea's Peter Bonetti.

Despite the loss of Banks, the game could not have started better for England, who looked far sharper after their harder group matches. Charlton took command of the midfield, Terry Cooper burst forward at every opportunity and Hurst looked dangerous whenever he got the ball. Their superiority was soon reflected in the scoreline as, after 31 minutes, Mullery scored his only international goal after starting the move from well inside his own half of the field. Newton, who had laid on the goal for Mullery, then provided the cross for England's second on 50 minutes, which Peters gratefully snapped up to put his side 2-0 to the good and, playing their best football of the

above: The quarter-final: Bobby Charlton gained his record-breaking 106th cap, while England were beaten 3-2 by West Germany after leading 2-0. During the match, Hottges lunges in on Charlton while Alan Ball looks on.

right: Peter Bonetti, seen here at the training ground, was called up at late notice to keep goal against West Germany. Although he played well he carried most of the blame for the defeat, due to his error with the first German goal.

tournament, seemingly on their way to the semi-finals.

However, the Germans pulled themselves back into the game with a goal out of nothing. Beckenbauer's right-footed shot from the edge of the box crept in under the body of the diving Bonetti. Ramsey was not unduly worried as his side continued to dominate with the minutes ticking away, the 100-degree heat draining the strength from both sides. With one eye on the semi-finals, the England manager pulled off Charlton and Ball and sent on Hunter and Bell. The two he had substituted had been responsible for stifling the German midfield – and in particular Beckenbauer –

but now the white-shirted Germans were better able to penetrate the England half. The two sides traded close chances then, with just eight minutes remaining, a lapse in concentration in the England defence allowed Seeler to claim the equalizer with a bizarre backward-headed goal which looped over a surprised Bonetti.

The game went into extra time. The Germans, reinvigorated by their comeback, looked the fresher and, despite Hurst's disallowed 'goal' after just a couple of the extra 30 minutes, they always looked the likelier of the two sides to score. Sure enough, three minutes into the second period of extra time, Grabowski crossed for Lohr to flick on and Muller volleyed home from four yards, giving Bonetti no chance: West Germany 3 England 2. England had no answer as Charlton, one of England's greatest players and an obvious choice for the all-time England dream team, watched from the bench in what were the final minutes of his England career. His team went out of the tournament in the most dramatic and heartbreaking of circumstances. It was to be twelve long years before England would once again play in the World Cup finals.

Partly as a result of this amazingly tense game, Mexico 1970 grew in stature as a memorable World Cup. In the semi-finals West Germany were beaten 4-3 by Italy, with five goals coming in extra time, while Brazil beat Uruguay 3-1 to set up a mouthwatering final between two free-scoring sides. It was Pele, Rivelino, Jairzinho, Tostao and Gerson against Riva, Rivera and Boninsegna. Both countries had won the Jules Rimet trophy twice before and so the victors would win the golden statue outright.

With the score at 1-1 at half time, the Brazilians turned up the power in the second half and swept aside the Italians with an awesome display of

Kick-off time for the England *v.* Scotland encounter in 1971. Bobby Moore shakes hands with Bobby Moncur.

attacking football. Pele had headed his side into the lead during the opening period with Brazil's 100th World Cup finals goal and Gerson, Jairzinho and the team captain, Carlos Alberto, added three in the second half to make the final score 4-1 to the Brazilians.

In Mexico, it was fair to say that England had come closest to matching Brazil in a head-to-head game. Yet that fact was forgotten as England returned, dejected. The remaining four years of Ramsey's reign were to be overshadowed by that one game against West Germany and that single tactical error, taking off Charlton and Ball. The opinion that Ramsey's best was now behind him began to be voiced.

After the World Cup, England had just one game, a friendly against East Germany, before their first European Championship qualifier in Malta. Ramsey used the game against the Germans, which England won comfortably 3-1, to give a first cap to Leicester City's promising young goalkeeper, Peter Shilton.

The schedule of qualifiers for a quarter-final place in the 1972 European Nations Cup was kind to Ramsey as he was able to play Greece and Malta, the latter twice, before taking on the Swiss, England's main rivals for the one place in the knock-out phase. England were spared embarrassment in Malta by Peters, who scored the only goal of a game which England were expected to win by a cricket score. A 3-0 win over Greece was followed by a 5-0 win at Wembley against Malta and victory in the Home Championships to bring to a successful 1970/71 season to an end.

The two crucial games against the Swiss followed in October and November 1971. In Basle, England produced their best performance for some time to win 3-2. The return at Wembley ended in a 1-1 draw and, with a 2-0 win in Athens to follow, England went through to the last eight.

1972 EUROPEAN NATIONS CUP
GROUP THREE FINAL TABLE

	P	W	D	L	GF	GA	P
England	6	5	1	0	15	3	11
Switzerland	6	4	1	1	12	5	9
Greece	6	1	1	4	3	8	3
Malta	6	0	1	5	2	16	1

The quarter-finals were played on a two-leg basis and, seemingly inevitably, England were paired against West Germany, with the first leg to be played at Wembley. It was billed as a crunch tie: the Germans had avenged the World Cup final defeat of 1966 by winning in Mexico in 1970 and now a third meeting would determine which of the nations' sides was dominant. With England unbeaten in the eleven games since they last met, Ramsey remained loyal to the core of his World Cup-winning players, including five of the 1966 XI in the line-up:

Banks (Stoke City), Madeley (Leeds United), Hughes (Liverpool), Bell (Manchester City), Moore (West Ham United), Hunter (Leeds United), Lee (Manchester City), Ball (Everton), Chivers (Tottenham Hotspur), Hurst (West Ham United), Peters (Tottenham Hotspur).

The Germans were below strength following a bribe scandal but, despite this, still managed to comprehensively beat England, the game ending

above: Peters, Clarke and Channon surge forward whilst McGrain of Scotland attempts to cover. England beat Scotland 1-0 in this game played in May 1973.

left: Martin Chivers came into the attack following good form with Tottenham Hotspur. In total he won 24 caps and netted 13 goals.

3-1 to the visitors. The result was a hammer blow to Ramsey and his team. It was the first time England had lost at home to a German side and also the first time they had been beaten at home by more than one goal since the Hungarians had demolished Winterbottom's team in 1953. Needless to say, the second leg a month later in Berlin was a formality and, although England managed to avoid defeat, the 0-0 draw was of little consolation. The Germans went on to beat first Belgium, hosts for the semi-finals and final, and then the USSR to take the trophy for the first time.

The two-year cycle of World Cup and European Championship was now clearly the priority for England, while the Home Championships, so long the staple diet of British international football, was quickly becoming relegated to a sideshow. From 1967, when Scotland had embarrassed the world champions, England had dominated the encounters between the two. From the late 1960s to the mid-1970s, England also held sway over the Welsh and Irish. In 25 games against the home countries between 1968 and 1975, England won 16 and lost just 2.

The focus for Ramsey was now the 1974 World Cup. In England's qualifying group were Wales and one of Europe's strongest sides, Poland. Against the Welsh, England scraped home 1-0 in Cardiff but were held 1-1 in the return match at Wembley. Wales beat the Poles 2-0 and then Poland beat England by the same score in

Chorzow. The game was a nightmare for Moore, whose own goal and all-round performance showed that his best days at international level were now behind him. To add to Ramsey's worries, Ball was sent off. Only one team would qualify from the group, the competition was still wide open with just two games left.

In the penultimate game Poland beat Wales 3-0 and now needed just a draw from the final group match, at Wembley, to qualify at England's expense. England warmed up for the crucial showdown with an emphatic 7-0 victory over Austria at Wembley and Ramsey decided that the same side would be the one to win the Poland tie and take England to West Germany and the 1974 World Cup finals.

Captained by Peters, Ramsey's team totally dominated the game – possibly like few others in his eleven-year reign as England manager. Yet his side's superiority was to count for nothing and England were to be unceremoniously dumped out of the World Cup, largely thanks to the Polish goalkeeper, Jan Tomaszewski, who had been dubbed 'a clown' by Nottingham Forest manager Brian Clough before the game.

During the course of the match more than a dozen clear goal-scoring opportunities fell to England's forwards. Mick Channon hit the post from three yards – one of two shots to hit the woodwork – while the Poles cleared from their own goal-line no fewer than four times. This did not include the numerous saves by Tomaszewski, some of which were not the least bit elegant, but all were effective. The Poles had come to defend and, if possible, cause England problems on the break. As England pressed with little over 30 minutes remaining, the Poles' counter-attacking game plan worked as Lato dispossessed Hunter on the halfway line and set off down the open expanse of the left wing. His low cross was met by Domarski, whose first-time strike nutmegged Hughes, England's remaining defender, deceived Shilton and ended up in the back of the England net.

England hit back within six minutes as Peters was fouled in the Polish penalty box and Clarke converted the spot kick to level the scores. But Poland continued to soak up England's pressure. The minutes ticked by, the crowd looked to the England bench for an injection of new blood, but Ramsey did not stir. The game had entered its 87th minute when he finally made a change, sending on Kevin Hector for Martin Chivers for the Derby County winger's first taste of international football. The swap almost paid off as Hector headed a last-minute corner goalwards only to see it cleared from the line, and Clarke following up could only stab his reflex shot wide. It was England's last chance. The 1-1 result meant that, for the very first time, England had failed to qualify for the World Cup finals.

1974 WORLD CUP QUALIFYING
GROUP FIVE FINAL TABLE

	P	W	D	L	GF	GA	P
Poland	4	2	1	1	6	3	5
England	4	1	2	1	3	4	4
Wales	4	1	1	2	3	5	3

The finals were dominated by the Dutch. Cruyff, the world's best footballer, aided by Neeskens, Rep and Rensenbrink, appeared to play a different game to everyone else. They beat defending champions

above: Alf Ramsey and his coaches at the training camp in January 1974 with Alan Ball getting all the attention.

left: Peter Shilton has things covered as Moore breaks forward in England's 0-1 defeat by Italy, November 1973.

Brazil, then Uruguay, Argentina, Bulgaria and East Germany on their way to the final. Their opponents in the final were the West Germans who, under Beckenbauer, had started the tournament poorly but now looked worthy finalists having overcome the Poles in the second phase.

The final opened dramatically, with English referee Jack Taylor awarding a penalty to each side inside the first half hour. Then Gerd Muller, playing in his last international, put the hosts 2-1 ahead before the break. It was a lead the Dutch could not respond to and so the Germans won the title for the first time since 1954.

The blame for England's failure to qualify for the 1974 World Cup fell rightly or wrongly onto the shoulders of Sir Alf. The man who had won the World Cup for his country had been under pressure since England's defeat by West Germany in the Mexico World Cup four years before and

now the calls for his head became ever louder. Ramsey was in charge for just two more games after the draw against the Poles: a 1-0 defeat at Wembley against Italy in November 1973 and a 0-0 draw in Lisbon against Portugal the following April.

The records show that Ramsey was in charge of England for 113 games over nine years, winning 69 times, drawing 27 and losing 17. The friendly against Italy marked another notable goodbye as Moore, Ramsey's World Cup-winning captain and one of England's greatest players, wore the white shirt for the last of his 108 games. Like Billy Wright before him, Moore also captained his side 90 times.

In Ramsey's place came the former Manchester City boss, Joe Mercer, acting as a caretaker manager while the FA looked for a longer-term replacement. His first major responsibility was the

above: Kevin Keegan fires in a rasping volley in the Home Championship game against Wales at Ninian Park, Cardiff, in May 1974. Bell, McFarland and Channon are in attendance. England won the match 2-0.

left: The FA, who had no prospective candidate lined up to succeed Alf Ramsey, appointed the genial Joe Mercer as a stand-in.

Home Championship campaign, in which England shared the honours with the Scots. Mercer then took the England side on a European tour in the summer of 1974. His reign lasted just three short months during which England played 7 games, winning 3, drawing 3 and losing just 1, against the Scots.

On 4 July 1974 the FA announced the name of the new England manager. To no-one's surprise it was to be Don Revie, the man who had pulled Leeds United from the depths of the Second Division and turned them into one of the most feared teams in Europe. The former Manchester City and England insideright, who had scored 4 goals in his 6 international games, was now in the England hotseat.

Revie's first season, 1974/75, could not have gone better for England. His first game was a crunch European Championship qualifier against England's main rivals for a place in the finals, Czechoslovakia, at Wembley. He called up Gerry Francis, the attacking midfield general from Queens Park Rangers, for his debut and made him captain of his first line-up:

Clemence (Liverpool), Madeley (Leeds United), Hughes (Liverpool), Dobson (Burnley), Watson (Sunderland), Hunter (Leeds United), Bell (Manchester City), Francis (Queens Park Rangers), Worthington (Leicester City), Channon (Southampton), Keegan (Liverpool).

After a slow start to the game, it took the introduction of another Queens Park Rangers player, winger Dave Thomas, to turn the game England's way and the 90,000 crowd were sent home in good voice as two goals from Colin Bell following an opener by Channon saw England get

above: Mick Channon missed with this effort but scored later in the 3-0 defeat of Czechoslovakia at Wembley, October 1974.

left: Don Revie becomes the new England team manager in July 1974 and quickly gets down to demonstrating what he expects from his players.

their campaign off to a flying start, winning 3-0. Portugal held a disappointing England 0-0 in the second qualifier a month later, then Revie's side pulled off an excellent 2-0 victory over world champions West Germany in a friendly to mark England's 100th Wembley match. One month later, Malcolm McDonald created a piece of history by becoming the first England player to score five goals in a full international in the post-war era, against Cyprus. England's next game was the return fixture in Limassol, where they managed just a single-goal victory. England finished the season with a famous win over the Scots, 5-1 at Wembley, in which captain Francis, returning to the side after injury, scored twice. It

was to be England's best performance under Revie.

In the European Championships England's fortunes took a dramatic turn for the worse. The Czechs demolished Portugal 5-0, which put a great deal of pressure on England, with crucial games in Bratislava and Lisbon coming up. England succumbed to the Czechs in the first, losing 2-1 and, after Portugal and Czechoslovakia drew 1-1, England were effectively out. They needed to beat Portugal by a hatful and hope the Czechs would slip up against Cyprus. It was too much to ask for as England's game in Lisbon ended in a 1-1 draw. After a bright start their campaign had run out of steam.

Pele turns out for the USA in a four-team tournament in America as part of the 1976 Bicentennial celebrations. Trevor Cherry has the task of marking the Brazilian, who appears to still take some stopping.

Gerry Francis, England's captain, meets up with Moore and Pele at the American Bicentennial Cup tournament.

1976 EUROPEAN CHAMPIONSHIP QUALIFYING GROUP ONE FINAL TABLE

	P	W	D	L	GF	GA	P
Czechs	6	4	1	1	15	5	9
England	6	3	2	1	11	3	8
Portugal	6	2	3	1	5	7	7
Cyprus	6	0	0	6	0	16	0

England had failed, but the Czechs were the form side of Europe and England's attempt at qualification had been a brave one. Their victors beat the USSR 2-0 in their quarter-final, then Holland 3-1 in a semi-final to set up a final against West Germany. For the first time a major international competition was decided on penalties as the game ended 2-2 after extra time.

The Czechs held their nerve and won the spot-kick competition 5-3.

While the focus of European football was on the finals, England went to the USA in the summer of 1976 to take part in a four-team tournament organized to help promote the game to the American public and celebrate the American Bicentennial. They lost to the Brazilians, beat the Italians and, in an unofficial game against a USA XI captained by Bobby Moore, finished with a win.

World Cup qualifiers were soon on Revie's mind. England had now failed to progress beyond the qualifying stage of an international tournament at two attempts and the press and fans were restless. Much was expected of Revie, yet he had so far been assessed as failing to deliver and, with some debatable team selections, left himself wide open to criticism – something which he had not experienced while at Elland Road.

The main obstacle to England's progress to Argentina and the finals of the 1978 World Cup

England failed to qualify for the 1978 World Cup, but did tour South America in 1977. This team played Argentina in June of that year. From left to right, back row: Neal, Hughes, Watson, Cherry, Wilkins, Clements. Front row: Pearson, Talbot, Keegan, Channon, Greenhoff.

was the Italians. After England had beaten Finland twice in their opening two qualifiers, 4-1 and 2-1, the crucial fixture in Rome loomed. For Revie, this was a make-or-break game as, if England were to lose, they would stand little chance of topping the group and his own position would surely become untenable. The England side, only five of which had played in England's previous game, the uninspiring win over Finland at Wembley, was:

Clemence (Liverpool), Clement (Queens Park Rangers), Mills (Ipswich Town), Greenhoff (Manchester United), McFarland (Derby County), Hughes (Liverpool), Keegan (Liverpool), Channon (Southampton), Bowles (Queens Park Rangers), Cherry (Leeds United), Brooking (West Ham United).

The Italians, who included seven players from Juventus, dominated the game from start to finish. In truth, England had travelled more in hope than belief and Italy won the game by a greater margin than the 2-0 result suggested. The *Daily Mirror's* back-page headline read 'Worlds Apart' and that said it all. Revie put on a brave face and refused to admit that England were effectively out of the running for a place in Argentina in 1978. The result left England a mountain to climb in the form of at least a 3-0 win over Italy back at Wembley.

England lost three out of their next four games, all at Wembley. The only victory was a 5-0 defeat of Luxembourg, but even in that game England were booed off at half time with the score at 1-0. England then lost to a Cruyff-inspired Holland – a game which only served to deepen the depression. They lost also to Wales and then Scotland, whose fans demolished the Wembley pitch following the

visitors' 2-1 win. England finished in third place in the Home Championships for only the second time since the war and, with the press on their backs in that summer of 1977, departed for a tour of South America.

However, the team travelled without their manager. Revie said that he was going to see Finland's game against Italy, which ended in a 3-0 win for the Italians. In fact, he was completing personal terms for a move to the United Arab Emirates, a departure which came as much of a surprise to the Football Association as it did to the public. On the field, England drew all three games of their tour, against Brazil, Argentina and Uruguay, but it was the manager's departure that made all the headlines.

Revie's record as England manager was poor in comparison to others who have taken on the job. In charge for just 29 games, under Revie's direction England won 14, drew 8 and lost 7. Revie had achieved so much with Leeds United, but later admitted himself that the unique pressures and demands of the England job had not suited him and the weight of expectation was too great. His departure from the England job tarnished his reputation and a life-long love of the game and his country until the day he died in May 1989.

The FA now had to look for a replacement. Choosing another maverick was out of the question, so they rejected the people's choice, the outspoken Brian Clough. Another leading contender, Bobby Robson, was enjoying success but was under contract with Ipswich Town. The FA needed to steady the ship, to make a conservative choice. They looked next to the football academy of East London: West Ham United.

PETER SHILTON
Leicester City/Stoke City/Nottingham
Forest/Southampton/Derby County
Goalkeeper
125 international caps (1970-1990)

If it is records you want, enter Peter Shilton. Having kept goal for the national side for nearly twenty years, he has more caps than any other England or European player. A remarkable 66 clean sheets during his tenure is the story of a complete goalkeeper. His last cap was in the third place play-off game in the 1990 World Cup v. Italy – after only a deflection in the semi-final had prevented him appearing in the final itself. Not a great showman but a great goalkeeper!

KEVIN KEEGAN
Liverpool/Hamburg/Southampton
Forward
63 international caps (1972-1982)

Twice voted European Player of the Year, Keegan had a natural talent to enthuse those around him. The 1970s were not the best times for the national side, but Keegan maintained a positive approach, earning him 63 caps and the captaincy on some 29 occasions. He did not always have a very harmonious relationship with the national team managers – clashing with Revie and Robson, but working well with Greenwood. This is a player who would have commanded even greater respect had he played in a more successful England side.

RAY WILKINS
Chelsea/Manchester United/AC Milan
Midfield
84 international caps (1976-1986)

Ray Wilkins came through the ranks at Chelsea and, as he matured to England status, he led a change in playing styles that had its roots in the Italian game. The poise over the ball, the passing sideways for safety when other options were limited and the calmness of the pass were his trademarks. This cultured approach to the play slowly became part of the English game and he gained recognition for that by amassing some 84 caps. Ironically, his last awards were gained whilst he was playing for AC Milan.

FOREVER
ENGLAND

Ron Greenwood's appointment as interim England coach in 1977 came as an accolade to an experienced and respected football authority.

Greenwood was not even the manager of West Ham at the time of his appointment – he had stood aside for John Lyall in 1974. However, Lancaster Gate viewed sixteen years at Upton Park as preparation enough for an England manager, despite the fact that the last couple of those years was spent away from the day-to-day running of the team. Not surprisingly, he felt he had been given a new lease of life with this most unexpected of appointments, but he was to repay that confidence in him by restoring some lost pride in the England team.

The three matches that Greenwood was initially employed to cover were a friendly against Switzerland and two World Cup qualifiers, against Luxembourg and Italy. He had two months to prepare for the first. He was fully aware that it was not just the public who were unsure of the direction the England football team was taking, but the players too. So, part public relations exercise, part serious fact-finding mission, the new England manager toured the big clubs of England putting forward his own

blueprint for the national side's future – and got an encouraging response.

The Swiss game, in September 1977, came after a run that had seen England fail to beat a top nation for over a year. Greenwood played safe with his selection and picked six Liverpool players from the team that had just won the European Cup, plus one ex-Anfielder in Kevin Keegan. The full side lined-up as follows:

> Clemence (Liverpool), Neal (Liverpool), Cherry (Leeds United), McDermott (Liverpool), Watson (Manchester City), Hughes (Liverpool), Keegan (SV Hamburg), Channon (Southampton), Francis (Birmingham City), Kennedy (Liverpool), Callaghan (Liverpool).

The major surprise was the inclusion of Ian Callaghan, whose recall to the England side after an eleven-year gap represented the longest period between caps of any England player in history. In a tight and largely uninspiring game, which saw Ray Wilkins come on for Callaghan and Gordon

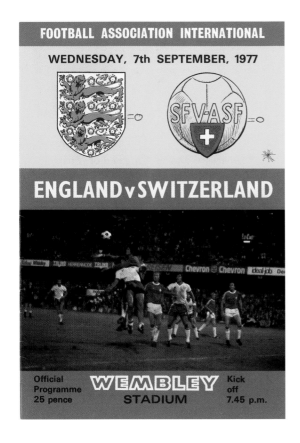

The England *v.* Switzerland game in September 1977 was Ron Greenwood's first match as the national team manager. The result was a 0-0 draw.

Kevin Keegan captained England in 29 of his 63 games.

Hill for Mick Channon, England could not break down a well-organized Swiss defence and had to settle for a 0-0 draw.

Greenwood's two subsequent trial games were more important. In the World Cup qualification programme thus far England had beaten Finland twice and Luxembourg once, but they had lost against Italy – who were easily the major threat to England's progress. This made it crucial for Greenwood's side to beat Luxembourg and then avenge the loss against the Italians if they were to have any chance of progressing to the finals. It

was a tall order and the team's over-eagerness showed in Luxembourg where England managed just a 2-0 win.

Meanwhile Greenwood had asked for, and got, wholesale changes to the structure of the England set-up. He called upon a number of top managers and coaches to look after England sides at all levels, surprisingly the first time this had happened. Bill Taylor and Geoff Hurst were retained to work alongside Greenwood with the senior team. Bobby Robson and Don Howe worked on England 'B' and Dave Sexton, Terry Venables and

opposite: Over his twelve-year tenure in the England shirt, Emlyn Hughes played under four different managers, gaining 62 caps and captaining the side on 23 occasions.

Howard Wilkinson took charge of the Under-21s. The Youth team went to the man who, for many years, many England fans wanted to see in the main job, Brian Clough.

On the field, Greenwood looked to build his side around Keegan. With 30 caps to his name, the Hamburg star was an inspiration to a generation of young hopefuls. The England manager had nothing but praise for the player later to go on and manage the national side, saying that he was 'the perfect example of a "self-made" footballer'.

The Italy match, in November 1977, was Greenwood's first big Wembley night, but England had to win – and win by a substantial margin at that. The Italians had beaten Finland 6-1 in their previous match, so had a superior goal difference to England and had just one game in the group left after the Wembley showdown, against lowly Luxembourg. To win was a tall order and the manager took the risk of bringing three new caps into the forward line. The night belonged to Keegan and Trevor Brooking, each scoring with the help of the other, as England overcame the Italians 2-0 in front of a 92,000 crowd.

It was a great effort by the England side and their performance, possibly the best of the 1970s, restored some lost confidence. However, Italy now had only to beat the minnows of Luxembourg to qualify for Argentina on goal difference at England's expense. This they did,

winning 3-0 in Rome. England's failure to qualify could not be attributed to the new manager and, to no-one's surprise, Greenwood was given the job on a permanent basis.

1978 WORLD CUP QUALIFYING GROUP TWO FINAL TABLE

	P	W	D	L	GF	GA	P
Italy	6	5	0	1	18	4	10
England	6	5	0	1	15	4	10
Finland	6	2	0	4	11	16	4
L'bourg	6	0	0	6	2	22	0

England had three friendly games plus the Home Championship tournament to navigate before the next qualifying competition began – for the 1980 European Nations Cup. Greenwood's main task was to use these games to build a side that would secure England's qualification for a major tournament for the first time in almost two decades. The captaincy of the side moved from Keegan to Emlyn Hughes, as Greenwood believed that an England captain should play in the Football League week in week out.

England lost to the West Germans and then drew 1-1 with Brazil. They then took the Home Championship with ease, winning all three games. The 1-0 win at Hampden Park was especially pleasing to the English as it was the Scots' final warm-up game before they departed for the 1978 World Cup finals in Argentina, where they were humiliated at the hands of Peru, Iran and the press.

England beat another World Cup qualifier, Hungary, 4-1 at Wembley to finish the season, but they could only sit and watch as Italy – the side which had pipped England in the qualifiers – beat the hosts and progressed to a place in the third-place play-off, which they lost to Brazil. In the final, Argentina beat Holland, losers now in two successive World Cup finals, 3-1 after extra time.

Greenwood, having made a fine start to his new job with 6 wins, 2 draws and just 1 defeat in his opening 9 games, now looked forward to the European Nations Cup qualifiers with some confidence. England were to win through to the finals in consummate style, winning 7 and drawing 1 of their 8 games.

Of the nations in England's qualification group, Denmark represented the greatest threat. The game in Copenhagen, the first of England's group matches, was a seven-goal thriller in which Keegan scored twice and Latchford once while Phil Neal added a fourth – the defender's third goal for England in just four games. This was quite a record considering only one goal had been scored by an England number two (Keith Newton against Malta) since Alf Ramsey netted a penalty in the infamous defeat at the hands of the Hungarians a quarter of a century before.

Also in England's group were the two Irish sides. Northern Ireland were beaten twice, 4-0 at Wembley and 5-1 at Windsor Park. The Republic side were also expected to be easily overcome but, inspired by Arsenal's Liam Brady, they held England at Lansdowne Road. Despite this stand, they were defeated at Wembley 2-0 in February 1980 in a game that saw the twenty-three-year-old Bryan Robson, at that time with West Bromwich Albion, make his international debut.

Potentially, England's most difficult remaining game of the series now looked to be in Sofia against Bulgaria but, on a hot summer afternoon,

above: October 1978 and the Republic of Ireland game was a qualifier for the 1980 European Championships. Cherry and Currie are competing in a practice match before the event, while Phil Neal looks on.

opposite: In March 1980, a visit by the English team to the impressive Nou Camp stadium in Barcelona resulted in a superb 2-0 win with goals from Woodcock and Francis.

opposite far right: Another fine 3-1 win, this time over the World Cup holders Argentina at Wembley, confirmed that England were making progress.

Greenwood's side came through, winning 3-0. The return match was postponed because of thick fog (this was the only England game at Wembley ever to be postponed). Keegan had commitments with Hamburg that caused him to miss the re-match, which was played the following day, but he was not missed. England won the game 2-0, which, after much pressure from the press and armchair England managers, saw the introduction of Tottenham Hotspur's Glenn Hoddle, who stepped onto the international stage for the first time and capped a fine performance with a 20-yard goal.

1980 EUROPEAN CHAMPIONSHIP
QUALIFYING GROUP ONE FINAL TABLE

	P	W	D	L	GF	GA	P
England	8	7	1	0	22	5	15
N. Ireland	8	4	1	3	8	14	9
Irish Rep.	8	2	3	3	9	8	7
Denmark	8	1	2	5	13	17	4
Bulgaria	8	2	1	5	6	14	4

The friendlies played during the run-in to the finals began with a creditable 2-0 win against a strong Spanish side in Barcelona, and then another win, 3-1, against world champions Argentina at Wembley. The Home Championship provided Greenwood with three games before his squad's departure to Italy. The first was against Wales. Greenwood rested six of his key players – with disastrous effect as the Welsh ran home 4-1 winners.

For the visit of Northern Ireland he brought back Ray Wilkins, Dave Watson and Emlyn Hughes. However, the 1-1 draw hardly restored confidence in the side and, with the visit to Hampden looming, England faced the distinct possibility of finishing bottom of the table. In front of a baying Hampden crowd, England confounded their critics and turned in a confident and well-organized display. Brooking netted an early goal to settle England's nerves and quieten the Scottish support, Coppell added a second in the second half and 88,000 Scots went home severely disappointed.

England's final game before the European championships was in Australia to commemorate the centenary of the Australian Football Association. It was a fixture that Greenwood could have done without so he sent a side of nearly-men on the periphery of his squad. The selection, which won the game 2-1, included four debutants. A fifth, Peter Ward of Brighton and Hove Albion, came on as a substitute in his one and only England game. Of the fourteen players who played (three substitutes were used), only Butcher, Robson, Hoddle and Mariner can claim to have had substantial England careers.

Eight nations qualified for the finals of the 1980 European Championships. England's group included the hosts, Italy, Belgium and Spain. Greenwood was confident that England might make the knock-out phase of the tournament. The opening match was against the Belgians and Greenwood fielded a predictable but experienced side:

> Clemence (Liverpool), Watson (Southampton), Thompson (Liverpool), Neal (Liverpool), Sansom (Arsenal), Wilkins (Manchester United), Brooking (West Ham United), Coppell (Manchester United), Woodcock (Cologne), Johnson (Liverpool), Keegan (Hamburg).

England began the game well. Woodcock had the ball in the net only to see it ruled offside against a Belgian side operating a tight offside trap before Wilkins broke the deadlock with a stunning individual goal. As the Belgians cleared an England attack, Wilkins picked the ball up just outside the penalty box. The Belgian defence rushed out but the England man chipped the ball over them, ran onto his own pass and coolly lobbed the ball over goalkeeper Pfaff to open the scoring. England's lead, however, was short-lived as Ceulemans took advantage of some slack England defending to level the scores at 1-1. This was instantly followed by trouble among England's supporters. The Italian police responded, firing tear gas into the England section of the crowd but the gas wafted down from the stands and onto the pitch, choking Ray Clemence in the England goal. The West German referee stopped the game and,

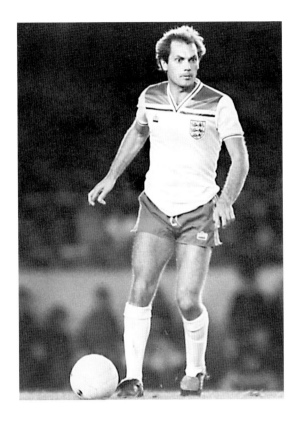

opposite page: Glenn Hoddle was in and out of the national side – some managers liked him, some didn't. All in all, however, he was a classy player who would go on to manage the England team.

left: Ray Wilkins had become one of the anchormen in the Greenwood set up: his ability to hold up play whilst instigating the next attack could prove unsettling for the spectators but reflected the changing face of international football.

been an influential figure in Nottingham Forest's two European Cup wins and now teamed up with his old partner, Tony Woodcock, to try to do for England what they had done for Nottingham Forest.

This was always going to be a tight game with few open scoring chances, so when Ray Kennedy's drive beat the legendary Dino Zoff in the Italian goal only to hit the post, many felt that the writing was on the wall for England. As Keegan was forced to play deeper and deeper, the Italians were able to stamp their authority on the game. The only goal of the match came from the home side. Graziani flew down the Italian left wing, leaving a despairing Phil Neal in his wake, and crossed low and hard. Tardelli, who had spent most of the game shadowing Keegan, ghosted into the England box and drove in a shot at the near post to claim the two points.

Luckily for England, Spain and Belgium played out a draw and so all four countries were still in with a chance of making it to the last four, although England's fate was out of their own hands. England had to beat Spain in their final game and hope that Belgium v. Italy did not end in a draw – if it did, both those teams would go through.

Greenwood shuffled his pack once more, bringing in Viv Anderson, Mick Mills and, most crucially, Hoddle, for their first taste of the action in Italy. The midfield of Wilkins, Hoddle and

on its restart, England were unable to reassert their dominance and the game drifted to its inevitable conclusion.

The problems off the field ruined the game on it. England's return to competitive football, their first big game for ten years, had been overshadowed by the behaviour of their fans. The FA was fined £8,000 but the effect on England's image was a far greater loss. England should have beaten Belgium, now they needed to succeed against the home team – a tall order as Italy had not been defeated at home for a decade. Greenwood brought in Shilton for Clemence, Gary Birtles for David Johnson and Ray Kennedy for Trevor Brooking. The surprise was the inclusion of Birtles – who had played just ten minutes of international football. However, he had

opposite: Ray Clemence and Peter Shilton: two fine goalkeepers who between them dominated the role for England over twenty years.

McDermott came together as an effective unit and between them provided an opening for Brooking, which he gratefully accepted to put England 1-0 up. The Spanish side responded with two penalties, both taken by Dani. He scored the first and then Clemence pulled off a remarkable save, from a re-taken spot kick, to keep the score at 1-1. Brooking, scorer of the first goal, turned into the instigator for England's winner. Instead of crossing a corner into the box, he pulled it back for McDermott, who drove in a fierce shot that Arconada could not hold, Woodcock drilling home the rebound.

Unfortunately for England, the Belgians and Italians duly played out the 0-0 draw that suited both sides and England returned home frustrated. They had created chances against Italy and could have beaten Belgium, but Greenwood had not come with a settled side that could unlock the tight, well-drilled European defences they encountered. The late introduction of the one man in the squad who might have been able to, Hoddle, was just that – late – and England had paid the price. However, in the light of events off the field, there were many that were not sorry to see the back of the Union Jack in the competition.

1980 EUROPEAN CHAMPIONSHIP
GROUP TWO FINAL TABLE

	P	W	D	L	GF	GA	P
Belgium	3	1	2	0	3	2	4
Italy	3	1	2	0	1	0	4
England	3	1	1	1	3	3	3
Spain	3	0	1	2	2	4	1

Belgium held the hosts to a 0-0 draw to win the group and progress to the final, where they met the Germans. Hrubesch put the West German side a goal to the good in the tenth minute. Their influential playmaker, Briegel, was substituted early in the second half, which allowed Belgium back into the game. Van der Eycken levelled the scores from the penalty spot only for Hrubesch to grab a last-minute winner for the Germans. England's European Championships experience was bittersweet, but it had whetted the appetite of the nation. England were finally back competing for the big prizes of international football alongside the top English clubs who were so dominant in Europe.

The next big test would be the 1982 World Cup in Spain. The format of the finals was changed once again as the competition was expanded to twenty-four qualifiers. From England's group, two of Norway, Switzerland, Hungary, Romania and England would make it.

The road to Spain began at Wembley with a creditable 4-0 win over Norway. It was the side's first game since Italy and, with Keegan unavailable, Robson was seen as the lynchpin at the heart of the England midfield. Eric Gates of Ipswich Town and Graham Rix of Arsenal earned their first caps as McDermott grabbed two of the goals.

However, Greenwood's men were to win just once in the next 8 games over the 1980/81 season, starting with a 2-1 World Cup reverse against Romania. England's bad patch spanned an unprecedented run of games at Wembley when they lost 2 and drew 3 of 5 matches. Qualification for España '82 began to look remote.

Political pressures forced the FA to abandon England's Home Championship game against

Northern Ireland as the IRA hunger strike grabbed the headlines. The Irish, under the management of Billy Bingham, had a strong side which stood a good chance of topping the table, whereas England were looking more like favourites for the wooden spoon. The cancellation meant that for the first time the tournament could not be completed.

Following a Wembley defeat by Scotland in May 1981, England travelled to Basle for a crucial World Cup qualifier against the Swiss. England had taken just 5 points from their 5 games and, with only four games remaining (two of them being against the much-fancied Hungarians), England needed at the very least to come away with a draw. Mick Mills was drafted back into the side to add some solidity to the defence, but England went 2-1 down and looked all but out of the running for one of the two qualifying places. On the flight from Switzerland to Budapest, where England were to play a second qualifier in a week, Greenwood contemplated retirement as England's manager. The criticism directed at him from the back pages of the press was clearly taking its toll, as it had done for Revie and Ramsey before him. Hungary were unbeaten so far and the game in the cauldron of the Nep Stadium represented a do-or-die situation for England, and Greenwood. The England line-up was as follows:

> Clemence (Liverpool), Neal (Liverpool),
> Mills (Ipswich Town), Thompson (Liverpool),
> Watson (Southampton), Robson (West Bromwich
> Albion), Coppell (Manchester United), McDermott
> (Liverpool), Mariner (Ipswich Town), Brooking
> (West Ham United), Keegan (Southampton).

Programme cover from England's visit to Romania for their 1982 World Cup qualifier.

The inclusion of Neal and Thompson was vital. Spirits were low in the England camp after the poor showing in Basle, but these two had just helped Liverpool lift the European Cup and were bubbling with enthusiasm. It infected the rest of the side as England held the Magyars at bay in the opening minutes of the game and then hit back themselves with a fine move which ended up with Brooking heading in a McDermott cross after 18 minutes. However, despite dominating the first half, an error by Ray Clemence allowed the Hungarians to equalize before the break.

Greenwood's England was not to be denied. The Man of the Match, Trevor Brooking, restored his side's lead with a ferocious volley after Keegan had set him up. Brooking was the key to England's success, but when he was substituted for Wilkins, the switch gave the home side a new set of problems to deal with. Finally, Keegan converted a penalty, after he had himself been brought down, to secure a fine 3-1 win. Greenwood responded by saying that the game had given him the greatest satisfaction of any in his career. Indeed that career was, he announced to players and press on the trip back to London, now at an end. Greenwood said that he wanted to step down from the manager's job but his

announcement was met with indignation from the squad – 'You're out of order. We want you to reconsider' said Keegan, reflecting the views of the other respected senior players. The view of the players was to see the job done and to review the situation at the end of the qualifying series. Greenwood, somewhat reluctantly, agreed.

If Greenwood had known in advance the result of England's next game, the side's first of the 1981/82 season, he might not have agreed to change his mind. England went to Oslo to play Finland in the seventh of their eight qualifiers. Robson gave England an early lead but disaster struck as first the home side drew level and then took the lead. England failed to respond and suffered the humiliation of losing to a soccer minnow. The team was a laughing stock and Greenwood took the brunt of the criticism.

England looked to be out of the World Cup – the two places would now surely go to Hungary

The England team line up prior to kick-off for the match against Hungary in November 1981, which they won 1-0 with a goal from Mariner. From left to right: Keegan, Shilton, McDermott, Thompson, Mariner, Coppell, Neal, Martin, Robson, Mills, Brooking.

and Romania. But succour came from an unexpected source as Switzerland took three out of four points from the Romanians to open the door for England. A draw in the final game of the series, at Wembley against Hungary, would see England get to Spain. Hungary had already qualified but England would pip Romania if they avoided defeat. The Hungary game sold out within days of Switzerland's 0-0 draw with Romania and the disaster of Oslo could be forgotten with just one last effort.

The hype before the game was not matched by the 90 minutes of football. The Hungarians, overawed by the atmosphere at Wembley, never looked interested in anything other than avoiding total humiliation. Paul Mariner scored the only goal of the game and England would compete in Spain after a roller-coaster ride through qualification.

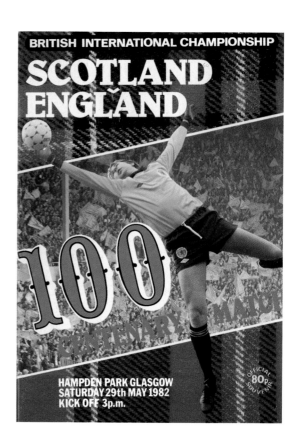

BRITISH INTERNATIONAL CHAMPIONSHIP

SCOTLAND
ENGLAND

100

HAMPDEN PARK GLASGOW
SATURDAY 29th MAY 1982
KICK OFF 3p.m.

Following the first international match in 1872, England and Scotland met for the 100th time at Hampden Park, Glasgow, on 29 May 1982. England defeated their old adversaries 1-0.

1982 WORLD CUP QUALIFYING
GROUP FOUR FINAL TABLE

	P	W	D	L	GF	GA	P
Hungary	8	4	2	2	13	8	10
England	8	4	1	3	13	8	9
Romania	8	2	4	2	5	5	8
Switzerland	8	2	3	3	9	12	7
Norway	8	2	2	4	8	15	6

Greenwood could not have asked for more from his players from the time England qualified for Spain to the first group match in Bilbao against the French. A fine 2-0 win over Holland at Wembley supplemented maximum points from the Home Championships, which included a 1-0 win in Glasgow in the 100th encounter between the English and the Scots. Greenwood also took a full England side to Bilbao in March to play a friendly against Athletico. The game ended in a 1-1 draw, but as a public relations exercise the trip proved invaluable. England's final two warm-up games saw a first match against Iceland, ending in a 1-1 draw, and a 4-1 win in Finland. England departed for the finals to the sounds of their promise to their fans: 'This time, more than any other time… We're gonna find a way… We'll get it right' was the lyric from the chart-topping single. They also had a seven-match unbeaten run

Steve Foster played in the 1982 World Cup finals for England. He only played in three games, but no goals were scored against his defences – a tribute to his determination and commitment.

under their belts, their last reversal being the debacle in Oslo.

The team's departure coincided with the retaking of the Falkland Islands, and the strong bonds between Spain and Argentina made England's presence at the World Cup awkward for their hosts. There was talk of Spain refusing to let England play, of the Argentines pulling out if England were allowed to play and the fear of what might happen should the two countries meet in the latter stages of the tournament. Flags proclaiming 'First The Falklands, now the World

Cup' adorned many of the ships returning from the South Atlantic. However, all fears of violence proved unfounded. The two countries did not meet and there were few signs of anti-English sentiments whenever Greenwood's side played. This was undoubtedly helped by the fact that England played their group games in Bilbao in the Basque country. Had England been due to start the tournament in Madrid things might have been different.

England's manager had problems of his own as two of his key players, Keegan and Brooking, were carrying injuries. Both travelled to Spain but neither could expect a game in the opening phase of the competition. England's first match, in a group also including Czechoslovakia and Kuwait, was against France. In Keegan's absence, Mills was handed the captaincy for Greenwood's 50th game as England manager. The England side lined-up as follows:

Shilton (Nottingham Forest), Mills (Ipswich Town), Sansom (Arsenal), Thompson (Liverpool), Butcher (Ipswich Town), Robson (Manchester United), Coppell (Manchester United), Wilkins (Manchester United), Mariner (Ipswich Town), Francis (Sampdoria), Rix (Arsenal).

England made a dream start to the game with a set-piece move that could not have worked better on the training ground. Almost immediately from kick-off they won a throw-in on the right side of the pitch and level with the French box. It was launched into the danger area by Steve Coppell, Terry Butcher back-headed and Bryan Robson stormed into the box, unmarked, to volley past Ettori in the French goal to score the fastest goal

above: The 1982 England squad selected for the World Cup finals. From left to right, back row: Robson, Woodcock, Foster, Hoddle, Withe, Anderson, Brooking. Middle row: Coppell, Rix, Thompson, Clements, Corrigan, Shilton, Butcher, Francis, Wilkins. Front row: Sansom, McDermott, Mariner, Keegan, Mills, Neal.

left: The posters for Spain 1982 show World Cup Willie had become Bulldog Billy.

in World Cup history, after 27 seconds: England 1 France 0. The French gradually pulled themselves back into the game and, after 25 minutes, equalized through Soler, and so it remained until half-time.

Platini and Giresse were the French danger-men and they had shown glimpses of their combined genius in the opening 45 minutes. Now Greenwood switched his side around to allow Robson and Wilkins to threaten the French and snuff out their creative ability. This worked and it was England who grabbed the initiative in the second half. After 66 minutes Robson added a second with a powerful header from a Francis cross. Mariner added a third as England dominated the rest of the game to send a clear message to the other main contenders – West Germany, Brazil, Argentina and Spain – that England were not to be taken lightly.

Another 40,000-plus crowd turned up for England's second game, against Czechoslovakia. Greenwood's side looked less fluid, despite creating a number of chances in the opening period and the sides went in at the break 0-0. Robson, suffering from a groin strain, was substituted for Hoddle. It took almost another twenty minutes for England to break down a solid Czech defence when Francis was on hand to punish the Czech goalkeeper, who could not hold a Wilkins shot. Barmos then deflected a Mariner cross into his own net to give England a deserved 2-0 win.

By the time England came to face Kuwait in their final group match, qualification for the second phase was already secure. The game was won 1-0 thanks to a Francis goal and England, like Brazil, came through with a 100 per cent record from the first round of group matches. There was some concern at the side's inability to convert chances, especially as they now faced much tougher competition, but the team could not have done better. And there was always the prospect of Keegan and Brooking returning.

1982 WORLD CUP GROUP FOUR
FINAL TABLE

	P	W	D	L	GF	GA	P
England	3	3	0	0	6	1	6
France	3	1	1	1	6	5	3
Czech.	3	0	2	1	2	4	2
Kuwait	3	0	1	2	2	6	1

Through to the second phase, along with Northern Ireland, who had also topped their group, England were now drawn in one of the four groups of three teams, the winners of which would progress to the semi-finals. The few days of rest before the first Group B match against West Germany gave Keegan and Brooking extra time to regain match fitness. It now emerged that, after the Czech game, Keegan had flown to Hamburg to see a specialist about his back. He had borrowed the car of the receptionist at the hotel where England were staying and at one o'clock in the morning – with the agreement of his manager – driven 250 miles to Madrid to catch a flight to Hamburg. Keegan returned four days later pronouncing himself fit for action.

However, Greenwood did not risk Keegan for the German game but instead fielded the same eleven that had beaten Czechoslovakia. A crowd of 75,000 packed into the Bernabeu Stadium in Madrid for the clash but it singularly failed to live up to its pre-match billing. Both sides showed too much respect for the other and, apart from a raking drive from Rummenigge that crashed against Shilton's cross-bar with just five minutes remaining, neither side looked liked scoring.

West Germany then beat Spain 2-1, so now England had to go one better against the host country. On a night of frustration for England, a second 0-0 draw sent the Germans through to the semi-finals. The Spanish goalkeeper, Arconada, was by far the busier of the two but England could not find the finishing touch to end some promising moves, with Francis and Robson both coming very close to opening the scoring. With 18 minutes left, Keegan and Brooking came on for Rix and Woodcock and instantly added an extra dimension to England's attack. Both had good chances to score, particularly Keegan who headed wide when it had seemed easier to put the ball into the net, but England's World Cup ended in frustration. England had started the tournament against the French looking bright and inventive; they finished it seemingly unable to score.

above: Brian Robson and Terry Butcher celebrate the second goal against France in the 1982 World Cup. Battison is the player looking on.

left: Trevor Brooking should probably have received more than the 47 caps he got. A great entertainer and brilliant reader of the game – perhaps he was a bit too nice as a player!

1982 WORLD CUP SECOND STAGE
GROUP B FINAL TABLE

	P	W	D	L	GF	GA	P
W. Germany	2	1	1	0	2	1	3
England	2	0	2	0	0	0	2
Spain	2	0	1	1	1	2	1

Elsewhere, the Italians, who had started the tournament in very poor fashion, suddenly came to life and beat both Argentina and Brazil to claim a place in the last four. Rossi scored both goals in the 2-0 semi-final win over Poland and, in the most exciting and controversial game of the tournament, West Germany beat France on penalties after the game had ended 3-3. Italy then beat West Germany 3-1 in the final to clinch the World Cup for the third time.

England's game against Spain brought an end to the Greenwood era. The man who had taken over the hotseat in 1977 with England at a low ebb had achieved a degree of success. He now stepped down in July 1982 to be replaced by the England 'B' team coach and Ipswich Town manager, Bobby Robson. Greenwood had been in charge for 55 games: England had won 33, drawn 12 and lost 10.

BRYAN ROBSON
West Bromwich Albion/Manchester United
Midfield
90 international caps (1980-1992)

'Mr Perpetual Motion' Bryan Robson was a player who could win the ball, pass the ball and score great goals – he was not called Captain Marvel for nothing! First capped in 1980, he represented England over the next twelve years, gaining 90 caps – being captain in 65 of those games. Robson's 26 international goals from midfield is a testimony to his enthusiasm and his ability to read a game and he holds the record for the fastest-ever goal scored in the World Cup finals. If he had not been so prone to injury, his already impressive record would have been even better.

TERRY BUTCHER
Ipswich Town/Glasgow Rangers
Central defender
77 international caps (1980-1990)

Terry Butcher was an old-fashioned centre half who managed to excel playing the modern game. He was 6ft 4in tall, over 14 stone and not the fastest defender around. Despite this, he was one of the best, with excellent positional play and bravery that was second to none. His debut against Australia in 1980 was followed by a further 76 caps. Butcher is one of few players to have played in three World Cup final competitions – 1982, 1986 and 1990, where he made his last appearance for England in the semi-final against West Germany.

Bobby Robson's appointment as England's new team manager was widely welcomed by players, press and public.

England's first match under the guidance of Robson was in Denmark, where they drew 2-2. This image from the game shows Terry Butcher moving in for a tackle on Preben Elkjaer.

The choice of Bobby Robson as the new England manager was widely accepted. He had been involved in the England set-up prior to his appointment, while his success at Ipswich Town was every bit as impressive as Ramsey's prior to his step-up to the England job. As a player, Robson had gained 20 caps and 4 goals in an England career spanning four years.

Robson's reign as England manager began with controversy. There was no room for the thirty-one-year-old Kevin Keegan in his squad. Keegan captained England 29 times out of 63 appearances and scored 21 goals, but, as far as Robson was concerned, his time was up. Keegan, securing a midfield slot in England's all-time line-up, would return to the England set-up as manager seventeen years later.

Robson's reign began with an away fixture against Denmark in September 1982 – England's first game in their bid to secure qualification for

the 1984 European Championships. Trevor Francis gave England a dream start with a goal after seven minutes but, with 20 minutes remaining, the home side equalized. England hit back, again through Francis, and were set for an unlikely victory when Olsen levelled the scores in the dying seconds of the game. A 3-0 win in Greece was followed by a 9-0 home win over Luxembourg and, at Christmas, England were in pole position. However, in their next game Robson's side dropped a vital home point against Greece, while Denmark kept winning.

The Home Championship of 1982/83 saw England beat Wales and Scotland, while only drawing with Northern Ireland. England then embarked on a three-match summer tour of Australia and, with a return of a single win and two draws, Robson had much to ponder before his side's showdown with Denmark. England v. Denmark came while there were still seven matches in the group to play. It was a game England had to win, but they lost 1-0. Despite winning their remaining two games, England lost out on qualification to Denmark by just one point.

1984 EUROPEAN CHAMPIONSHIP QUALIFYING GROUP THREE FINAL TABLE

	P	W	D	L	GF	GA	P
Denmark	8	6	1	1	17	5	13
England	8	5	2	1	23	3	12
Greece	8	3	2	3	8	10	8
Hungary	8	3	1	4	18	17	7
L'bourg	8	0	0	8	5	36	0

France warmed up for the finals with a 2-0 win over England in a Paris friendly in February 1984. They were the favourites to win the title and they delivered. They beat Denmark in the group phase before beating Portugal in an epic semi-final. The final saw France take on Spain. In an entertaining game, Platini and Bellone scored to win the game 2-0.

Prior to the finals, the 1983/84 Home Championship campaign was contested. This Home Championship was to be the last, 100 years after it – the world's oldest league programme – had been contested for the first time. Until the 1950s this series of games was a highlight in the football calendar but, when the teams began competing in the World Cup, its importance steadily waned. Then, when the European Championships grew to incorporate all the footballing nations of Europe, the pressure became too much. The Home Championship had to be sacrificed.

The final games saw England beat Northern Ireland 1-0 at Wembley, then lose 1-0 to the Welsh in Wrexham before drawing 1-1 with the Scots in Glasgow. As befitting the final Home Championship tournament, each side won one game, drew another and lost one, resulting in a fitting four-way tie.

1983/84 HOME CHAMPIONSHIP FINAL TABLE

	Pd	Wn	Dn	Ls	GF	GA	Ps
N. Ireland	3	1	1	1	3	2	4
Wales	3	1	1	1	3	3	4
England	3	1	1	1	2	2	4
Scotland	3	1	1	1	3	4	4

A 2-0 home defeat by the USSR followed and, with Europe gearing itself up for the championships, England departed for a tour of South America – never a happy hunting ground at the best of times, least of all with confidence at rock bottom. The Portsmouth striker Mark Hateley had been one of few players to catch the eye against the USSR when he came on as a substitute with 20 minutes remaining, so Robson gave him his chance in the first game of the three-match tour, against Brazil in Rio. In the team that day was another youngster, Watford winger, John Barnes. The game would change both players' lives.

England started brightly, perhaps relieved to be away from the spotlight at home and, as half time approached, the 0-0 scoreline looked like being a real bonus. However, Terry Fenwick hit a long ball from defence which found Hateley in the inside left position. Hateley flicked the ball wide to Barnes. Forty yards from goal and with the entire Brazilian midfield and defence in front of him, Barnes saw a gap and cut inside three players. Now on the edge of the penalty area, another

left: A famous goal scored by John Barnes was the highlight of a great 2-0 victory over Brazil in Rio de Janeiro in June 1984.

opposite: Gary Lineker would emerge from the 1986 World Cup with the Golden Boot and a much-enhanced reputation.

burst of speed took him across the face of the goal and, leaving defender after defender in his wake, Barnes was now confronted with the goalkeeper. With a confidence that belied his tender age, he didn't snap a shot goalwards but drew the goalkeeper into a dive before taking the ball out of his reach and burying in into the net. It was a stunning individual goal that belonged in the Maracana, and was recognized by the Brazilian press as one of the best ever scored against Brazil in the great stadium.

Both sides appeared evenly matched in the second half but it was England who drew blood again as Barnes crossed for Hateley to climb high above the Brazilian defence to head home. There was no fightback from the home side and England won the game 2-0 to record probably their best result in a friendly match since the 1930s – if not of all time.

England followed up this win with a 2-0 defeat in Uruguay and a draw in Chile, but when the squad came home, the country was still buzzing from the win over Brazil. For the young Barnes the pressure to repeat that wonder goal – his first for his country – each time he played for England was immense and unfair, while for Hateley his contribution led to a move from the English Second Division to European giants, AC Milan.

The Brazil game also transformed the fortunes of the side as they began their assault on qualifying for the 1986 World Cup. England started with an emphatic 5-0 win over Finland at Wembley and never looked back. England's first ever game against Turkey ended in an 8-0 rout in Istanbul. They remained unbeaten throughout the programme – unique among all qualifiers for that tournament – securing their place with a second 5-0 win, this time over Turkey, when Gary Lineker scored a hat-trick.

At the end of the 1984/85 season, and with three World Cup qualifiers left to play, England were invited to Mexico to take-part in a four-team tournament. They lost their opening game against Italy, then lost to the hosts before beating West

Programa Oficial.

$ 300.⁰⁰

ESTADIO AZTECA
Junio 2/15 1985

This colourful programme reflects the flags of the nations taking part in the 1985 Mexican tournament.

1986 WORLD CUP QUALIFYING
GROUP THREE FINAL TABLE

	P	W	D	L	GF	GA	P
England	8	4	4	0	21	2	12
N. Ireland	8	4	2	2	8	5	10
Romania	8	3	3	2	12	7	9
Finland	8	3	2	3	7	12	8
Turkey	8	0	1	7	2	24	1

England were seeded for the finals in Mexico because they had won the 1966 World Cup, although they had, in the intervening two decades, scarcely looked like repeating that feat. However, this meant Robson's side would avoid the tournament favourites in the opening phase of the competition.

England's group matches were to be played in Monterrey and the opening game was against an unfancied Portugal side. The day before the game the England doctor, Vernon Edwards, was admitted to hospital after suffering a heart attack, while among the players the fitness of the England captain, Bryan Robson, was the concern of every fan and journalist following England's build-up to the opening game. Bobby Robson threw a shroud of secrecy around his captain and, on the day of the game, Robson led the side out. The full England team lined up as follows:

> Shilton (Southampton), Stevens (Everton),
> Sansom (Arsenal), Hoddle (Tottenham Hotspur),
> Fenwick (Queens Park Rangers), Butcher
> (Ipswich Town), Robson (Manchester United),
> Wilkins (AC Milan), Hateley (AC Milan), Lineker
> (Everton), Waddle (Tottenham Hotspur).

Germany 3-0. The team returned home via the USA, although this time England added a further game to their schedule, a first official fixture against Canada. They beat the USA 5-0 in Los Angeles and then won 1-0 against the Canadians.

England's final qualifying game for the World Cup was against Northern Ireland at Wembley. England had already booked their place for Mexico following their rout of Turkey, now Billy Bingham's side needed a point to join England in the finals. A packed Wembley was in festive mood and, perhaps only slightly tongue-in-cheek, both sets of fans were singing 'It's a fix' as the game drifted to an accommodating 0-0 draw.

In the 1985 pre-World Cup tournament in Mexico, this England squad played Italy, losing 1-0. From left to right, back row: Francis, Shilton, Wright, Hateley, Waddle, Butcher. Front row: Sansom, Wilkins, Robson, Steven, Stevens.

The game was a disaster for a previously in-form England. The Portuguese took a surprise lead (ending Peter Shilton's remarkable record of not conceding a goal in World Cup finals since the opening game of the 1982 tournament, a run totalling 499 minutes), then Robson fell heavily on his injured shoulder. Clearly in agony, he was replaced by Steve Hodge, the Aston Villa midfielder. England regrouped and Hateley missed a good chance to put England into the lead. Portugal's Carlos Manuel did score, in the 75th minute, to finish off England.

The England manager took a pounding from the press after the defeat but kept faith with the same XI for the game against Morocco. As in the first game, England sweated but could not break down the Moroccan defence. When captain Robson hit the ground with a thud and did not get up again, the omens for England were not good. Obviously in great pain, Robson was again helped from the field and, for the second game, replaced by Hodge. Worse was to follow as England's frustration began to build. Acting captain Ray Wilkins, responding to a decision

Brian Robson shoots in spite of a determined challenge from a Portugese defender during the 1986 Mexico World Cup.

from the referee, picked up the ball and threw it in the direction of the man in black. Wilkins was sent off – becoming the first England captain to get his marching orders and the first England player to be dismissed in World Cup finals. England hung on for a point and a 0-0 draw.

England were now on the verge of their worst World Cup display since 1950. Manager Robson, now without his captain and vice-captain, looked to a more fluid line-up for a match he had to win – and win well. Lineker and Peter Beardsley, England's two key strikers, were to link up for only the second time. The worst fears of fans were swept aside during a first-half display which left the Poles gasping to keep up and the rest of the

world looking on at a rejuvenated England. Hoddle and Hodge mastered the midfield and, in Beardsley, Robson had found the perfect foil for Lineker. After just eight minutes England produced a team move of rare quality. Hoddle began it, Gary Stevens provided the cross and Lineker the finish. Within ten minutes the England striker had volleyed in his second.

Lineker then tapped home a simple third from a Trevor Steven corner to complete his hat-trick and a more-than-satisfactory first half for England. For once, the large contingent of England fans had something to cheer about: well before the end of the game they were dancing around the stadium. Chelsea's Kerry Dixon came on for Lineker in the

Mark Hateley worked hard but with little success in this World Cup game against Portugal – Bento turns this attempt away for a corner.

second half and Chris Waddle did likewise for Beardsley, as manager Robson was now assured of the Lineker-Beardsley partnership. If they were to be England's secret weapon in the finals, Robson was not going to let future opponents see too much of it.

1986 WORLD CUP FINALS
GROUP F FINAL TABLE

	P	W	D	L	GF	GA	P
Morocco	3	1	2	0	3	1	4
England	3	1	1	1	3	1	3
Poland	3	1	1	1	1	3	3
Portugal	3	1	0	2	2	4	2

Round two saw England face Paraguay, who, in Romario, had one of the outstanding talents of South American football.

The England side were confident and, following two fine saves from Shilton in the first half hour, gradually imposed themselves on the game. Lineker opened the scoring before the break and added a second after 72 minutes. Sandwiched between the Lineker strikes was a goal from his partner, Beardsley. The 3-0 result was extremely satisfactory for England and the way it had been achieved earned Robson's side a new respect.

Through to the quarter-finals, England now faced Argentina. A crowd of 114,000 crammed

above: Gary Lineker had a magnificent game against Poland, scoring a hat-trick in the first half.

opposite: Gary Stevens and Trevor Steven rise together to thwart Zabala of Paraguay in the second round game of the Mexico World Cup.

into the Azteca Stadium in Mexico City to see another chapter in the eventful history of meetings between these two rivals. The sides were evenly matched and the first half produced few, if any, clear-cut chances. However, in the second period, one man turned the game – the Argentine number ten, Diego Maradona.

The talented but temperamental midfielder had only briefly threatened to expose the England defence as he had others in the tournament, but after 51 minutes he picked the ball up and found Valdano to his right on the edge of the England box. Hodge challenged the Argentine but mis-hit his clearance. The ball ballooned up into the England penalty area and Shilton raced forward to punch clear over a challenge from the diminutive Maradona. Maradona connected first and the ball ended up in the back of the England net. Shilton, incensed, claimed that Maradona had not headed the ball but punched it past him. There were few remonstrations from other England players and only with the assistance of replayed slow-motion television pictures and stills of the incident could it be clearly seen that Maradona had indeed handled the ball.

Four minutes later Maradona had the ball in the back of the England net for the second time, this time with a piece of individual brilliance that matched any other in the history of the World Cup. He picked the ball up in his own half and, with England defenders first backing off and then floundering in the tackle, charged his way to the England goal. Shilton tried to narrow the angle but, with Butcher sliding in a last desperate lunge, Maradona slotted the ball past the England goalkeeper to make the score 2-0.

England had paid their opponents too much respect and now, with the minutes ticking away, found themselves with a mountain to climb. Robson waited until the 74th minute before making a tactical substitution, bringing on Barnes for Steven. It transformed the game as Barnes began to do what no other England player had: take on and beat Argentine defenders and threaten the Argentine goal. In that final 16 minutes Argentina looked more vulnerable than in any other game on their way to lifting the trophy.

On 81 minutes Barnes crossed from the left and Lineker headed home his sixth goal of the tournament from within a crowded penalty area. Minutes later, in an identical move, the England number ten was within inches of connecting with another Barnes cross. With the goal at his mercy, suddenly a defender appeared from nowhere to distract the England man. His attempted header inched wide and England's World Cup was over.

Diego Maradona punches the ball past Peter Shilton to give his country the lead in the quarter-final of the 1986 World Cup.

After the game Maradona was asked about his handball goal, his response was that the goal was the result of 'The Hand of God'. England took their defeat gracefully and with admiration from many quarters: Pele was one of many to comment, saying that if the incident had been reversed then the Argentines would have 'trampled the referee'. Maradona went on to score both goals in Argentina's straightforward 2-0 semi-final win over Belgium, while the clash between France and West Germany for the other final place also ended in a 2-0 win, for West Germany. The final was a five-goal thriller, with the Argentine centre forward Jorge Burruchaga grabbing the winner in the closing minutes after the Germans had fought their way back from being 2-0 down to level the scores.

From the disasters of the opening two games, England returned home, if not bathed in glory, but holding their heads high. Robson now looked to the future and the European Championship finals

Lineker among the goals again: this time he scores in the 1-1 draw against Brazil at Wembley in May 1987.

of 1988, which were to be held in West Germany. England's qualifying group had them pitted against Yugoslavia, Turkey and Northern Ireland. A friendly against Sweden prior to their opening game had ended in defeat but had not dented England's self-belief and with two goals from Lineker, now with Spanish giants Barcelona, and one from Waddle in a comfortable 3-0 win over Northern Ireland, Robson's side was up and running. A 2-0 win over Yugoslavia in November 1986 was followed by an incredible display of goal-scoring by Lineker, who grabbed all four of England's goals in an exciting 4-2 friendly against Spain. This result was made even sweeter for

England's marksman as the game was played at the home of Barcelona's arch-rivals, Real Madrid.

Following a second victory over the Irish, with three games left to play, England needed just four points to qualify top of their group.

The visit of Brazil ended in a draw, this time 1-1. A second goalless draw in three games, against Scotland in Glasgow, was then followed in September 1987 by a comprehensive 3-1 beating in Dusseldorf. England may have been waltzing through qualification but there was clearly a gap between the Germans – hosts and favourites for the European Championships – and England.

Turkey's visit to Wembley allowed Lineker to clinch his second international hat-trick of the year as England notched up an eight-goal win. Then England travelled to Belgrade needing just one point to qualify ahead of their hosts, Yugoslavia. England's form in the qualifying group had been impressive, they had yet to concede a goal and had dropped just one point. However, they were to save their best for last and, for the first time, England registered a victory in Yugoslavia, winning by a comfortable 4-0 scoreline.

1988 EUROPEAN CHAMPIONSHIP QUALIFYING GROUP FOUR FINAL TABLE

	P	W	D	L	GF	GA	P
England	6	5	1	0	19	1	11
Yugoslavia	6	4	0	2	13	9	8
N. Ireland	6	1	1	4	2	10	3
Turkey	6	0	2	4	2	16	2

Following qualification England had a frustrating run of 6 games, winning 2 and drawing 4. They were held to a 0-0 draw by Israel, before a memorable 2-2 draw against Holland at Wembley and another 0-0 in Budapest, against Hungary. A 1-0 defeat of Scotland and a 1-1 draw against Colombia comprised England's performance in the first Rous Cup. Their final game before the championships saw England win 1-0 in Switzerland.

England's first Euro '88 match was against the Republic of Ireland, who were managed by one of England's heroes of 1966, Jack Charlton. Both sets of players were drawn from the same pool of English First Division players, yet while England's team looked jaded and lacking in creativity, the

above: England's team for the game against Hungary in April 1988. From left to right, back row: Anderson, Adams, Pallister, Lineker, Woods, Waddle. Front row: McMahon, Steven, Robson, Beardsley, Pearce.

opposite: After a rocky start, Tony Adams ultimately made 66 appearances for his country. An inspirational captain, he was tactically aware, very demanding and an excellent central defender.

Irish showed a level of commitment and verve that made Robson blush. His defence looked slow and unsure and, as early as the fifth minute, mistakes by Kenny Sansom and Gary Stevens left Liverpool's Ray Houghton the opening to beat Shilton and put the Irish into the lead.

England did not threaten a comeback until Robson replaced Webb with Hoddle with 30 minutes of the game remaining. However, the Irish held firm and pulled off a famous victory. England's defensive frailties and lack of potency in attack were both cruelly exposed and, with the clash with the Dutch approaching, Robson clearly had problems. Robson's enforced team changes reminded England followers of the do-or-die game in Mexico against Poland, but the Dutch were much more formidable opponents than the Poles.

In the first half, England played the better football but still found themselves a goal down. It took a typical Bryan Robson surge through the Dutch defence to bring England back into the game at 1-1. Inspirational though it was, Robson's goal did not prove to be a turning point. The brief England revival was punctured as van Basten added his second to restore his side's lead. Completing his hat-trick less than five minutes later, van Basten sealed England's fate.

The USSR and the Republic of Ireland had drawn their game, so although England were now effectively out of the tournament, any two of the three other sides could reach the second phase. For England the game with the Soviets would be a matter of restoring pride. But their performance was, if anything, of an even lower standard than the two previous ones and Robson's side was beaten 3-1. England's record at the 1988 European Championships was the worst of any England side at a major finals.

1988 EUROPEAN CHAMPIONSHIP
GROUP TWO FINAL TABLE

	P	W	D	L	GF	GA	P
USSR	3	2	1	0	5	2	5
Holland	3	2	0	1	4	2	4
Irish Rep.	3	1	1	1	2	2	3
England	3	0	0	3	2	7	0

The Dutch played West Germany in the first semi-final and came from behind to win 2-1. The USSR also won their semi-final, against Italy, to set up a second clash between themselves and Holland. Munich was a sea of orange as the Dutch took over the town for the final and the visitors were not disappointed as Gullit and van Basten scored in a convincing 2-0 win.

Robson's side was ridiculed on its return for a lacklustre showing. But the manager's head did not roll – probably because he had, by general consensus, chosen the right players. They were genuinely unlucky against the Irish, met the eventual winners on the top of their form and, when already out of the tournament, played a side who had to win to progress. Robson's next task was qualification for the 1990 World Cup, to be held for the second time in Italy. With two countries progressing to the finals, the obstacle of playing Sweden, Poland and Albania, was not considered to be insurmountable.

The opening game, at Wembley against Sweden, ended in a 0-0 draw and then England took maximum points from two games with Albania, winning 2-0 in Tirana and 5-0 at Wembley. When England beat Poland 3-1 at Wembley, the two unbeaten sides in the group looked firm favourites to qualify. They drew, 0-0 in Stockholm, and both teams had effectively qualified with four games still to play. England finished their programme with a third 0-0 draw, this time in Katowice against the Poles. It meant that they had qualified without conceding a goal, although Sweden finished as group winners.

1990 WORLD CUP QUALIFYING
GROUP TWO FINAL TABLE

	P	W	D	L	GF	GA	P
Sweden	6	4	2	0	9	3	10
England	6	3	3	0	10	0	9
Poland	6	2	1	3	8	5	5
Albania	6	0	0	6	3	15	0

The qualification for Italia '90 gets underway and a potentially difficult fixture in Tirana against Albania comes early in the schedule: England win comfortably 2-0. From left to right, back row: Butcher, Pearce, Waddle, Walker, Lineker, Shilton. Front row: Rocastle, Webb, Robson, Stevens, Barnes.

Shilton (Derby County), Stevens (Everton), Pearce (Nottingham Forest), Walker (Nottingham Forest), Butcher (Glasgow Rangers), Robson (Manchester United), Waddle (Marseille), Gascoigne (Tottenham Hotspur), Barnes (Liverpool), Lineker (Tottenham Hotspur), Beardsley (Liverpool).

England's preparations for the finals comprised seven games, six of them at Wembley, between November 1989 and June 1990. They drew 0-0 against Italy, beat Yugoslavia 2-1 and had a memorable 1-0 victory over Brazil, followed by a 4-2 win over Czechoslovakia. A 1-0 win over Denmark, a 2-1 defeat by Uruguay and a fortunate 1-1 draw against Tunisia on the eve of the tournament all helped Robson mould his side. The one question throughout was what to do with the enigmatic Paul Gascoigne. Robson clearly had a soft spot for the young Tottenham player, but could not bring himself to make Gascoigne an automatic selection. On many occasions since his debut Robson had either substituted him or brought him on midway through a game. However, Gascoigne's virtuoso performance against Czechoslovakia, where he made three and scored one of England's four goals, sealed his place as England's playmaker.

England began their campaign against Jack Charlton's Republic of Ireland side, who had become a bogey team for England in recent campaigns. The side for the opening game in Sardinia lined up as follows:

Lineker put England ahead after just eight minutes, but the game was ultimately a dull affair. The Irish, battling hard, eventually forced an equalizer through Kevin Sheedy as the game petered out into a 1-1 draw.

England now played the Dutch and, for the first time Robson adopted a sweeper system, using Derby County's Mark Wright in that position. Two years earlier the Dutch had severely exposed a flat England defence and this time Robson was not to be out manoeuvred. Gascoigne took control of the midfield, inspiring England to a fine all-round performance. Barnes, Robson and Lineker all had good chances, the latter having a goal disallowed (rightly) for handball. The Dutch, by contrast, had little to offer and even when David Platt replaced the injured Robson, England's domination continued. But a much-deserved goal did not arrive. In the last minute of the game, Stuart Pearce thundered a free kick past van Breukelen, but he had failed to see the referee signalling for an indirect free kick and England's jubilation at scoring a potential winner was short-lived.

The crowds gather for England's match against Holland, which resulted in a 0-0 draw.

Paul Gascoigne, an emerging talent who was to make a big impact during the 1990 World Cup finals.

After the Republic of Ireland's 0-0 draw with Egypt, each team in the group was on two points from two games and all had scored just once and let in one goal: things could not have been tighter going into the final two games. England had the best chance of progressing, playing the rank underdogs from Egypt. Robson put Wolverhampton Wanderers' highly-rated striker, Steve Bull, into the starting line-up for the first time. A year before, Bull had become the seventeenth and probably last England player to be selected while playing for a Third Division club, and celebrated

his call-up with a goal in the win over Scotland. However, it was a defender, Wright, who was to spare England's blushes. From a Gascoigne free kick on the left touchline, Wright rose above the defence to head home on 57 minutes, to register his one and only international goal. England held on comfortably to their 1-0 advantage to qualify for the next phase of the competition.

England qualified for the knock-out stages of the 1990 finals and were drawn to play the Belgians. With Robson injured the team was, from left to right, back row: Lineker, Barnes, Pearce, Wright, Shilton, Butcher. Front row: Gascoigne, McMahon, Parker, Walker, Waddle.

1990 WORLD CUP FINALS
GROUP F FINAL TABLE

	P	W	D	L	GF	GA	P
England	3	1	2	0	2	1	4
Holland	3	0	3	0	2	2	3
Irish Rep.	3	0	3	0	2	2	3
Egypt	3	0	2	1	1	2	2

England's opponents in the first knock-out round were Belgium, who had only beaten them once in eighteen attempts. Despite this historical advantage, Robson was under no illusions as to the task that faced his team, who were still without their captain – Robson had not shaken off the injury he picked up against Holland. The Belgians dominated the first 30 minutes of the tie, hitting the woodwork and having a strong penalty appeal turned down. It was not until half-time approached that England responded in kind when Barnes volleyed home a cracking shot only for his 'goal' to be (wrongly, as subsequent television replays showed) disallowed.

There was little to separate the two sides in the second half, apart from a second strike against the England woodwork, and, long before the referee blew for full time, it was clear that the game would probably require an extra 30 minutes, if not penalties. The first half of added time failed to produce a goal but, with both sides now apparently resigned to the sudden-death of the spot kick competition, England made one last effort with three minutes of the match remaining. Gascoigne made a final surging run at the heart of the Belgian defence and was pulled down 20 yards from goal. He took the resulting free kick himself, supplying a delicate chip into the box that Platt turned to his advantage. The England substitute, showing great poise, agility and skill watched the ball come over his shoulder and buried his right-footed volley into the back of Preud'homme's net. The Belgians had no response to this killer blow and England progressed to the quarter-finals.

England's last-gasp winner set up an intriguing match against the Cameroon. However, the Africans were no makeweights in the last eight. They had caused a real upset in the first game of the competition in defeating Argentina and, with a refreshingly cavalier approach, had gathered an appreciable legion of followers. It was against the run of play when England took the lead after 25 minutes through a David Platt header. At half-time Cameroon brought on their talisman, Roger Milla, and he was pulled down inside the England penalty box to give Kunde the chance to level the scores at 1-1 after 61 minutes. Far from resting on their laurels, the Cameroon side went in for the kill and, just four minutes later, took the lead through Ekeke.

With 15 minutes left and England looking increasingly desperate, Trevor Steven was brought on for Terry Butcher to shake the hold the Africans had on the game. By adding width to England's attack, Robson was attempting to pose some problems of his own. The match looked to be slipping away from England when, from nowhere, Lineker broke into the Cameroon penalty box and was clumsily felled before he could strike at goal.

David Platt volleys the ball into the Belgium net in the last minute of extra time and England move forward to the last eight.

Picking himself up from the ground, Lineker composed himself, sending the goalkeeper the wrong way to level the scores at 2-2.

For the second time in the knock-out phase, England were forced into extra time. Now, in a tense 30 minutes, they were rescued again by Lineker. In a repeat of the second goal, Lineker was pulled down inside the Cameroon's penalty box and, taking the kick himself, sent the goalkeeper the wrong way, this time to put his side, possibly undeservedly, into a winning lead. England's relief at the final whistle was clear for all to see. But for the Africans' inexperience at defending against a player of Lineker's quality, England would surely have been heading home instead of looking forward to a semi-final showdown against West Germany.

The first semi-final of the 1990 World Cup, Italy v. Argentina, served up an incomparable display of negative football and was settled on

above: Lineker scores with a well-placed shot past Illgner.

left: Gascoigne goes past Brehme and gets Augenthaler wrong-footed.

penalties, which the Argentines won. Twenty-four hours later, England and West Germany restored some credibility to the competition and continued the history of classic games between these two old adversaries.

The two teams were well matched. England were determined not to play second fiddle to their highly-fancied opponents and controlled a tight first half without really penetrating the German defence. The second period began in the same vein, but then England were struck a cruel blow. As the match was approaching the hour mark, the Germans won a free kick 20 yards from the England goal. Brehme struck a shot, which took a wicked deflection off the advancing Paul Parker, to loop high over a stranded Shilton and drop into the England net. It was a highly fortunate goal but England remained focused. Ten minutes from the end of the game they equalized. Parker crossed from the right and found Lineker on the edge of the German penalty area. Despite being surrounded by defenders, the England striker found room to

shoot, placing his left-foot drive past Illgner to level the scores.

The contest moved into extra time, during which both sides hit the post: Waddle for England and Buchwald for Germany. Then, as the minutes ticked down, Gascoigne dived into a strong tackle on the halfway line. England's young playmaker had already received a caution earlier in the competition, the Brazilian referee reached for his pocket and Gascoigne realized that if England were to win the game he would miss the final. Distraught, the England player appeared overcome with emotion and detached from the game. England fans in the stadium and the millions at home watched helplessly as England now seemed, momentarily, to be down to ten men. Lineker signalled to the bench to 'watch him', a dramatic moment caught on television, but there was no need for Robson to intervene. Gascoigne composed himself and the remaining minutes of the extra 30 were soon over and the second semi-final of the 1990 World Cup would be resolved on penalties.

England had never been involved in a penalty shoot-out before, while the Germans had learnt their lesson the hard way after losing the 1978 European Championship final to Czechoslovakia on spot kicks. After 120 minutes of football of the highest quality, there now followed just ten minutes of nail-biting drama. Would England emerge as heroes or would the prize fall to the Germans?

England went first and Lineker opened the shoot-out with a typically confident strike, which was matched by Brehme for West Germany. Then Beardsley and Matthäus both scored, then Platt and Riedle: 3-3. Pearce stepped up to take England's fourth but he drove his shot too close to Illgner, who saved with his legs. The Germans were now in the driving seat. Thon stepped up and scored, 4-3. Now Waddle had to score to keep England in the contest. He wasted no time in setting up the ball, returning to his run-up and striding in, but the pressure proved too much, his shot ballooning over the bar. Waddle's head dropped. As the rest of his German team-mates ran to their goalkeeper to celebrate their victory, Matthäus, the German captain, put his arm round Waddle to console the England player.

The England side, gathered in the centre circle, was in a state of shock. There were tears, and not just from Gascoigne. But, as the numbness slowly subsided, the overriding emotion turned to pride at England's achievement.

West Germany progressed to the final where they met Argentina in a repeat of the 1986 World Cup final. However, Argentina were a shadow of the side that had won that thrilling game and had been fortunate to have won through to the final in Rome. They set out to extinguish the German threat and, as many commented, played for penalties. The game was a bitter disappointment and won 1-0 by the Germans in normal time, ironically through a penalty.

England's semi-final defeat meant an extra game, the much maligned third-place play-off. Their opponents were the tournament's hosts, Italy. The game attracted a large crowd of over 50,000, who were well entertained by both sides in an even contest. The first half ended scoreless but Italy took the lead following a lapse of concentration by Shilton in the England goal. Playing in his 125th and final game for England,

right: Beardsley and the Italian goalkeeper Zenga collide during the third place play-off, which Italy won 2-1.

opposite left: Peter Beardsley goes to console Stuart Pearce after his missed penalty.

opposite right: Gascoigne, in tears, goes to salute the England fans.

Shilton rolled the ball towards the edge of his area but had not seen Baggio, who stole the ball from the England goalkeeper. A quick one-two with Schillaci presented Baggio with the chance to put his side into the lead – an opening that he gratefully accepted. Luckily for Shilton, Platt marvellously headed home a Tony Dorigo cross to level the scores. However, with just four minutes of normal time remaining, Parker was adjudged to have brought down Schillaci for a penalty to the home side. The Italian forward picked himself up and scored from the spot to claim his sixth goal of the tournament and win the Golden Boot.

The game ended in a 2-1 win for the Italians. But England had performed above anyone's expectations during the tournament and, rightly, Bobby Robson, in his last act as England manager, watched with pride as his team accepted their medals and joined the Italians in a deserved lap of honour.

England also said good bye to two heroes. This was forty-year-old Peter Shilton's final game for England. His international career spanned twenty years and he would have undoubtedly have amassed more than his total of 125 caps but for his rivalry with Ray Clemence. He kept 66 clean sheets for England, captained the side 16 times

(including this final game) and his tally of 17 World Cup performances is also an English record. Terry Butcher's last game in an England shirt had been in the semi-final against West Germany. Capped 77 times and captain on 7 occasions, Butcher had been a regular in the England side for many years. The abiding memory of the 6ft 4in man-mountain was probably his bandaged head and bloodied shirt on seeing England through to a World Cup finals: Butcher's passion when playing for England was never doubted.

Bobby Robson's tenure as England manager had finished on a high note for English football, although his record would not instantly suggest an era of England success. In charge for 95 games, England won 47, drew 30 and lost 18. When it mattered most, however, the team had played well and gone further in a World Cup than in any other apart from in 1966. When the squad returned from Italy, everyone from the manager down was a national hero. None more so than Gascoigne, whose performances had made him one of the stars of the tournament and whose tears struck a chord with every England fan.

GARY LINEKER
Leicester City/Everton/Barcelona/Tottenham Hotspur
Striker
68 international caps (1984-1992)

It was in May 1984 that Gary Lineker made his first appearance for the national team, but it was his sixteenth game that made his reputation as an exceptional striker. His three goals gave England a much-needed win in the 1986 Mexico World Cup match over Poland and set him off to winning the Golden Boot award as the leading striker in the tournament. He amassed a number of records during his international career and for six successive seasons he was England's top scorer. His total tally from his 80 appearances was 48 goals – just one short of Bobby Charlton's record.

PAUL GASCOIGNE
NewcastleUtd/TottenhamHotspur/Lazio/Glasgow Rangers/ Middlesbrough
Midfield
57 international caps (1989-1998)

A huge talent, he seemed to have uncanny skill with a football but rather less control on a controversial personal life. Born in Gateshead, he started his career with Newcastle United but moved on to Tottenham Hotspur at the age of twenty-one and soon gained his first cap. Suffering a severe injury in the FA Cup final in 1991 he was out of the game for a long period but ultimately was recalled by England in 1993. Over the span of nine years he was selected 57 times for his country, scoring 10 goals. A brilliant footballer, he was always high in enthusiasm and entertainment value.

STUART PEARCE
Nottingham Forest/Newcastle United
Full-back
78 international caps (1987-2000)

Known as 'Psycho' – a nicknamed gained from his very combative style of full-back play – Pearce is best described as committed but fair. However, you do not get 78 caps unless you also have ability and he had an abundance of that. Pearce possessed a tremendous shot from dead-ball situations, collecting 5 goals as a result and he had a fourteen-year period of selection for England that included 6 appearances at the World Cup finals in Italy in 1990.

TONY ADAMS
Arsenal
Central defender
66 international caps (1987-2001)

While Tony Adams had a troublesome private life, his football activities were outstanding. Following a first cap in 1987 he initially struggled to maintain a presence in the national side but, after his early casual selections, he became an automatic choice in his later days. His leadership qualities – well known at Highbury – eventually transferred to the England side, where he gained a great reputation as a captain of the national team and as an individual who led by example. Selection over fourteen years is a testimony to his resilience and determination.

CHAPTER**EIGHT**

THREE LIONS ON THEIR SHIRT 1990-1996

Appointed in the summer of 1990, Graham Taylor was the new manager of the England football team. He had worked wonders at Watford and done well at Aston Villa, but could he deliver for England?

Bobby Robson's public image during and after those finals days in Italy made the task for his successor, Graham Taylor, tough. Taylor's managerial record with Watford and Aston Villa was good, if not spectacular. He attempted to make up for his relative lack of experience by surrounding himself with those who had it. The ex-Southampton manager, Lawrie McMenemy, and World Cup winner, Alan Ball, were his lieutenants who would help him see England through to the European Championship finals in Sweden in the summer of 1992.

Taylor had just one game, against Hungary, before England were launched into the qualifying tournament. They won that, 1-0, before they faced the Republic of Ireland, Poland and Turkey – three opponents whom England had faced all too often in recent years. The first game saw England beat Poland 2-0 at Wembley with goals from Gary Lineker and Peter Beardsley. Taylor juggled his side for the next game, in Dublin, and England emerged with a point. The sides drew the rematch at Wembley, their third successive 1-1 scoreline. Then, after England beat Turkey 1-0 in Izmir, England saw daylight between themselves and their Irish rivals for the one place in the finals.

Following a 3-1 win over the USSR and a 2-2 draw against the visiting Argentines, England departed on a 1991 summer tour, an ambitious trip to Australia, New Zealand and Malaysia. They won 1-0 against the Socceroos, 1-0 and 2-0 against the Kiwis and, in the sweltering heat of Kuala Lumpur, beat Malaysia 4-2 in a game where Lineker netted all four goals. This feat took him above Jimmy Greaves's record of 44 goals from 57 internationals and within sight of Bobby Charlton's England scoring record of 49 goals from 106 games.

England began the 1991/92 season poorly. They lost 1-0 at home to the Germans and, back

Two young Southampton players – Le Tissier and Shearer – who went on to gain full international honours.

The match in Poznan did not go according to plan. The Poles took a deserved first-half lead and, as the minutes ticked down, were now themselves in the group's top spot. However, with just thirteen minutes of the game remaining, England won a corner. David Rocastle took it, Gary Mabbutt headed it on and England's captain, Lineker, scissor-kicked the ball home from four yards to level the scores and send England to the finals.

1992 EUROPEAN CHAMPIONSHIP QUALIFYING GROUP SEVEN FINAL TABLE

	P	W	D	L	GF	GA	P
England	6	3	3	0	7	3	9
Irish Rep.	6	2	4	0	13	6	8
Poland	6	2	3	1	8	6	7
Turkey	6	0	0	6	1	14	0

Eight teams won through to Sweden and England were grouped with the hosts, France and Yugoslavia. With only the cream of Europe in the draw, Taylor could not grumble at England's fate.

England fared well in the countdown to the finals. They ended France's long unbeaten run in February 1992, a game that marked the debut of Southampton's centre forward, Alan Shearer. England then drew against Czechoslovakia and the CIS and beat Hungary. England's final game before departing for Sweden was against Brazil. Gary Lineker had announced the end of his international career and this was his final home appearance. The England captain was cheered every time he touched the ball but failed to edge closer to Charlton's England scoring record in the 1-1 draw. England's goal that day came from David Platt, while Lineker missed a penalty.

in the European Championships, were then booed off after a 1-0 win over Turkey at Wembley. The win did, however, mean that England would go into their final game, in Poland, firm favourites to qualify. As Taylor announced his squad for the game in Poznan, Bryan Robson announced his retirement from international football. An England Youth and Under-21 player, Robson had made his first-team debut in 1980, and when he stepped out against Turkey months before, he had registered 90 caps and scored 26 goals for his country. That game was to be his last, as he was not selected for the Poland game.

On the eve of the tournament, injuries hit England's final preparations. First, Taylor was robbed of Gascoigne, then Arsenal's Lee Dixon. Taylor had left a place in his party of twenty for John Barnes, who had only played sporadically throughout the season, but Barnes lasted just a few minutes of a disastrous last warm-up game against Finland and was ruled out. Then Gary Stevens, the Glasgow Rangers right-back, sustained an ankle injury which ruled him out. Taylor faced the prospect of entering the finals with eighteen fit players. Luckily, UEFA allowed him to call up QPR's Andy Sinton and Manchester City's Keith Curle as last-minute additions to the squad.

Taylor's problems didn't end there. Liverpool's Mark Wright would now take no part in the opening group matches. Wright, having already upset the England manager for staying with his FA Cup-winning side instead of joining the England party the day after the Cup final, had sustained an injury, which Taylor only knew of after the squad had been announced. This time the England manager was refused the chance to call up a replacement and so was forced to take with him a player who would be unlikely to contribute.

Taylor was suffering an acute dose of the same mix of problems that had beset all his predecessors, namely too much domestic football, not enough time with his players and the perception that, in everything, club came before country. He echoed the sentiments of every England manager saying, 'What has happened in the last few days has not concerned me because the withdrawal of three players is nothing new. I've had this for twenty months now because of the absolutely ridiculous system we operate in our country as regards giving international football and international footballers

September 1991 and Paul Merson wins his first cap for England in the match against Germany.

any sort of priority. For me, it's a constant theme.'

The enforced changes meant Taylor had no choice but to play a largely experimental line-up for England's opening game, against Denmark in Malmo on 6 July 1992:

Woods (Sheffield Wednesday), Curle (Manchester City), Pearce (Nottingham Forest), Keown (Everton), Walker (Sampdoria), Palmer (Sheffield Wednesday), Platt (Bari), Steven (Marseilles), Smith (Arsenal), Lineker (Tottenham Hotspur), Merson (Arsenal).

England began tentatively during a largely sterile first half. Platt and Trevor Steven had settled into the game well, but clearly missing a genuine replacement for Gascoigne, England looked predictable. In attack, Lineker looked isolated, unable to trouble the Danish defence.

The Danes were unlucky not to win the game in the second half, hitting England's post with the best chance of the match. For Taylor the post-match enquiry after the 0-0 draw was uncomfortable: his injury-hit team looked decidedly average in what would be a tough group. England's second game was against the highly-rated French. Their manager, Platini, was able to select some of the best players in Europe: Papin, Boli, Deschamps and Leeds United's Eric Cantona were in the side,

while he chose to leave the exciting Perez on the bench for the first half. Taylor rung the changes. Switching to a sweeper system, which was alien to most of his own side, he brought in Shearer, David Batty and Sinton.

The game exploded into life with an X-rated Stuart Pearce challenge on Papin in the first minute but drifted to a 0-0 conclusion. The French came closest to breaking the deadlock only to see Sinton clear from his own goalline. At the end of the 90 minutes, both sets of fans booed their teams from the pitch following an instantly forgettable game. The hosts had beaten Denmark in the other Group One game, so instilling some life into what had been a stale tournament thus far, and now Sweden faced an England side in desperate need of a win.

Martin Keown, 43 caps. Rugged, determined and very competitive, he is the sort of player you want on your side.

Taylor's side gave him the sort of start England had not produced for many a game when, after just four minutes, Platt gave England the lead. The travelling army of England's fans, some of whom had, yet again, been making the wrong sort of headlines of their own, finally had something to cheer with the goal. Good chances then fell to Daley and Sinton to extend England's lead before the break and, had one been converted, a place in the semi-finals would have beckoned. However, it was not to be.

On 52 minutes the Swedes drew level through Eriksson. The crossbar thwarted the same player just seconds later but the tide had turned, emphatically, in Sweden's favour. On 62 minutes, Taylor then substituted Lineker. England's most prolific goalscorer since Bobby Charlton, Lineker, like Charlton before him, would now spend the remaining minutes of his international career on the England bench. Arsenal's Alan Smith replaced Lineker but it was the home side that struck the decisive blow with the best move of the game. The diminutive Brolin, playing two one-twos, drove a fierce shot past Chris Woods with just eight minutes remaining.

Taylor's first major test as England manager ended in failure and controversy. England had scored just 1 goal in 3 games and, apart from the first half against Sweden, had looked a journeyman side, not prospective winners. Ill-luck with injuries in the run-up to the competition played its part but few commentators and fans were happy with his team selections and none could forgive Taylor for his treatment of Lineker.

Lineker retired from the international game at the top. He began his England career quietly but burst onto the world stage with his six goals in the 1986 World Cup finals which won him the Golden Boot and his record of 48 goals from 80 games for England puts him into England's all-time dream team.

1992 EUROPEAN CHAMPIONSHIP
GROUP ONE FINAL TABLE

	P	W	D	L	GF	GA	P
Sweden	3	2	1	0	4	2	5
Denmark	3	1	1	1	2	2	3
France	3	0	2	1	2	3	2
England	3	0	2	1	1	2	2

It was scant consolation for Taylor but another fancied side, France, also fell at the first hurdle. Denmark, who had come into the finals as a late replacement for Yugoslavia, won their semi-final and then in one of the biggest upsets in European Championship history, beat Germany in the final. A battered Taylor now looked to the World Cup in 1994, which was to be hosted by the USA. England's qualifying group comprised old foes Poland, the emerging Norway, group favourites Holland, Turkey again, and San Marino.

In England's opening game Platt's goal saved England's blushes in a 1-1 draw with Norway. Two home wins followed, first over Turkey when Gascoigne scored twice in a 4-0 win, and then over San Marino when Platt scored four in an otherwise unconvincing 6-0 win.

Following a 2-0 win in Turkey, England faced a crunch match at Wembley against Holland. Gascoigne marshalled England into a 2-0 lead with goals from Barnes and Platt and all was looking good for Taylor's side. But his playmaker took a heavy blow to the face and did not emerge

June 1993 and England are in the USA. Paul Ince captains England for the first time as they beaten 2-0 by the host nation.

for the second half. Holland dominated the remainder of the game, which ended in a 2-2 draw. This was a blow to England's chances of qualification but worse was to follow as England could only draw 1-1 with the Poles and then suffered a 2-0 defeat in Oslo. Even second place in the group was looking increasingly unlikely.

In anticipation of qualifying for the World Cup finals the following year, the FA had arranged a short tour of the USA in the summer of 1993, following the two qualifying games. However, not only was England's participation in the finals now very much in the balance but the tour began in the worst possible way with a 2-0 defeat against the host nation. A 1-1 draw against Brazil was followed by a 2-1 defeat against Germany, bringing England's dismal season to a close.

England had to win their final three qualification games to stand any chance of returning to the USA. Goals from Les Ferdinand, Gascoigne and Pearce secured a 3-0 win over Poland in the first. England then played Holland. The game turned on a two-minute spell in the first half. Platt, bearing down on the Dutch penalty area, appeared to be bundled to the ground by Koeman. England's pleas for a penalty were turned down, the referee adjudging that the first contact was made outside the box. England were

above: England v. Holland – a game of great controversy. The match hinged on two incidents involving the Dutch centre-back, Ronald Koeman. This photograph shows the first of them as David Platt, the England midfielder, is bearing down on goal just before being cynically fouled. The offence was almost certainly worthy of a sending-off: the referee did not agree.

left: Minutes later and Koeman scores direct from a free kick and the game went away from England.

also shocked as Koeman, clearly the last defender, was not red-carded for the foul. England's free kick led to nothing, the Dutch broke and won a free kick of their own on the edge of England's box. Koeman stepped up and curled the ball over the wall and past a despairing David Seaman. It was a devastating blow from which England never recovered. Bergkamp added a second, England were out of the World Cup and Taylor was out of a job.

If that were not bad enough, salt was rubbed into the wounds in England's final qualifying game, against San Marino. England conceded an opening goal in the first minute of the game, without an England player touching the ball. Although they recovered to score seven themselves, the humiliation of that opening minute on top of the failure to qualify was too much and the England manager stepped down at the end of 1993. He had been in charge for 38 games. England had won 18, drawn 13 and lost 7 – a return not dissimilar to his predecessor Bobby Robson – yet, like many England managers before him, his failure in the key games was Taylor's main downfall.

1994 WORLD CUP QUALIFYING GROUP TWO FINAL TABLE

	P	W	D	L	GF	GA	P
Norway	10	7	2	1	25	5	16
Holland	10	6	3	1	29	9	15
England	10	5	3	2	26	9	13
Poland	10	3	2	5	10	15	8
Turkey	10	3	1	6	11	19	7
San Marino	10	0	1	9	2	46	1

The finals were a great success, attracting over three million spectators to the 52 games. On the field the matches were free-flowing. Brazil, the favourites, and Italy won through to the final.

Manager Graham Taylor – not normally a man to react aggressively – is furious over the Koeman incidents and vents his despair on the FIFA official.

Terry Venables took over as England coach in early 1994 and quickly set about the job, using his man-management and coaching skills to full effect.

However, the game was one of the worst of the tournament. After 120 minutes, the score was still 0-0 and the World Cup was settled, in Brazil's favour, on penalties.

The FA's search for a replacement for Taylor led them to Terry Venables who had, for many years, been one of the favourites to take on the England post. Venables had represented his country at every level, although was only capped twice, while playing for Chelsea in 1964. His managerial career began with Crystal Palace before he moved across London to Queens Park Rangers. There then came a surprise move to Barcelona where he won the Spanish championship and took his side to a European Cup final. A return to London and FA Cup success with Tottenham Hotspur followed.

Although Venables was recognized across the game as one of the country's best coaches, the FA's decision was not made easy by allegations relating to his business dealings. In the end these reservations led the FA to give Venables a shorter contract than he might otherwise have expected.

As hosts for Euro '96, England had automatic qualification and Venables was faced with the prospect of two years of friendly matches. His first game, against Denmark, ended in a 1-0 win and then England demolished World Cup finalists Greece 5-0. A 0-0 draw against Norway ended the season as the eyes of world football focused on the World Cup.

The USA, Romania, Nigeria and Uruguay visited Wembley during the 1994/95 season and England remained undefeated, albeit against less-than-world-class opponents. Venables' only away game was held in Dublin, but trouble inside the stadium following an early Irish goal led to the game being abandoned.

In the summer of 1995, England invited Sweden, Japan and Brazil to compete for the Umbro Cup. Venables' side came from behind to draw against Sweden, were unconvincing in victory against Japan and were well beaten by Brazil, who took the trophy back to South America. Venables now had nine games to prepare his side for the championships as the 1995/96 season began. It had became clear to the

The USA team made their first visit to Wembley in September 1994 and gave a decent performance while losing 2-0. Here, John Barnes closes in on Tom Dooley with Shearer pursuing.

Stuart Pearce rises up to clear a Hungarian attack during England's 3-0 win at Wembley in May 1996.

manager that there was no substitute for competitive football and, although England only conceded two goals and remained unbeaten during these games, the team's performances were sometimes little better than average.

Just weeks before the finals were due to begin, England went on a short trip to the Far East. The manager had not seen eye-to-eye with the FA over the arrangements for the trip, which including an official game against China and a run-out against a Hong Kong XI, but went along with what was little more than a public relations exercise. Both games were won but it was the activities of the players in Hong Kong that grabbed the headlines. Gascoigne in particular attracted much unwanted attention from the press.

Back in England, the country was going football crazy. For the first time in thirty years, England was hosting a major soccer tournament. England's three group matches were to be played at Wembley. The games had been sold out for over a year, while the build-up to each England game inside the old stadium was unprecedented as the home crowds in festive mood sang along to all the England team songs, from 'Back Home' to the Euro '96 chart-topping anthem 'Football's Coming Home'.

England's first game, and the tournament's opener, was against Switzerland. Venables left out his captain and top scorer, Platt, while sticking with Shearer – who had not scored a goal for his country in fourteen games. Captained by Adams, England lined up as follows:

Seaman (Arsenal), G. Neville (Manchester United), Adams (Arsenal), Southgate (Aston Villa), Pearce (Nottingham Forest), Anderton (Tottenham Hotspur), Ince (Inter Milan), Gascoigne (Glasgow Rangers), McManaman (Liverpool), Sheringham (Tottenham Hotspur), Shearer (Blackburn Rovers).

The opening spectacular for Euro '96 was a colourful welcome to the top football nations of Europe.

England's fans were rewarded with a bright start. Steve McManaman looked dangerous and had a chance to open the scoring, as did Darren Anderton and Gary Neville, but the Swiss goalkeeper, Pascolo, and his defenders kept their hosts at bay in the opening stages of the game. It took a move involving Ince and Gascoigne to free Shearer on the right who closed down on goal. The England number nine created space for himself, set his sights and drove in a low and hard right-footed shot that went into the Swiss net off the right-hand upright. Shearer, and then Sheringham, both had good chances to extended England's lead before the break while, at the other end, Grassi showed that the Swiss were not to be discounted with a shot that cracked against Seaman's crossbar from six yards.

England continued to control the game from the restart. Looking for the elusive second goal and wanting to give others needed experience, Venables brought on Barmby, Platt and Stone in place of Sheringham, Gascoigne and McManaman. But it was the Swiss who scored the second goal of the game when Pearce was very harshly judged to have handled the ball – a connection which appeared to be involuntary – and Tyrkyilmaz converted the resulting spot kick. England pushed for the winner in the final minutes of the game only to rely on a world-class save from Seaman to avoid what would have been an embarrassing defeat.

England had a week to mull over the disappointment of the result and the sluggishness of their overall performance. Their cause was helped when their other group opponents, Holland and Scotland, also drew, 0-0, and then Holland beat Switzerland 2-0 before England took to the field again, against the Scots.

The build-up to this one game was unequalled, with most England fans recalling memories of the

A typical Alan Shearer response to scoring – this one was his first goal of Euro '96.

tartan army spurring on their side to upset the English. However, as Wembley filled up, for once, England would be the better supported. The game began in a fast and furious fashion with little pattern emerging and no team dominant. Spencer had the first chance of the game for the Scots while two Sheringham headers represented England's best opportunities of a goalless first half. Venables rang the changes at half-time, aware that failure to win would severely dent the chances of his team lifting the trophy. Jamie Redknapp came on for Pearce while England's wide men, McManaman and Anderton, switched wings. The changes bore fruit as, on 52 minutes, Shearer headed home a Neville cross. McCoist

came on for Spencer and had an immediate impact, claiming a penalty following a Neville tackle. His calls were waved away by the Italian referee. Minutes later, when Durie went down after a challenge by Adams, he was more accommodating. All eyes were now on McAllister as he struck his penalty well but Seaman, diving to his right, made a marvellous save, parrying the ball to safety and a corner.

The resultant corner came across and was collected by Seaman who quickly released the ball to Anderton as England counter-attacked. Anderton found Gascoigne who was being closely shadowed by Hendry. In a moment of sheer genius, Gascoigne lobbed the ball over the Scots' captain, turned, leaving Hendry for dead, and as the ball came down, volleyed an unstoppable shot into the Scots' goal. His celebrations, mocking the 'Dentist's Chair' episode that had clouded England's pre-tournament Far East trip, were no more outrageous than the goal he had just scored. With just eleven minutes remaining, England's second goal, scored by a Glasgow Rangers player, was the hammer blow that beat the Scots.

Now England just needed a point against Holland to progress to the knock-out phase. England's record against the Dutch made disappointing reading: no win since 1982 and just 1 victory in 6 games at Wembley. However, they began the game in a positive frame of mind, which ultimately secured a marvellous victory and one which Venables himself said was the most pleasing of his tenure.

Having conceded penalties in their two previous games, England now got one of their own when Ince was brought down by Bild after 23 minutes. Shearer calmly slotted home the spotkick. The Dutch responded as the minutes ticked down to half time, Berkamp getting their best opportunity only to head wide. The turning-point of the game came in just the sixth minute of the second half when Sheringham headed England into a 2-0 lead from a corner. The goal sapped the energy from the Dutch while the delirious crowd lifted England's game to new heights. Before the hour mark, England extended their lead further. McManaman combined with Gascoigne in move that provided Sheringham with a shooting chance central to the Dutch goal. Unselfishly, he laid the ball on to an unmarked Shearer who drove an unstoppable shot past van der Saar: 3-0 to England. Within five

minutes England got their fourth as Sheringham followed up an Anderton shot to bag a brace. The Dutch had been run ragged by a goal-hungry England but managed to breach their opponents' defence with a little over ten minutes remaining, through Kluivert.

That consolation goal made little difference to England but it meant success for Holland and misery for Scotland. The Scots were winning their final group game against Switzerland 1-0 and news of England's demolition was being well received in the Scots' camp. However, Kluivert's late strike reversed the two countries' fortunes and dealt the Scots a cruel blow; Holland now qualified for the next phase on goal difference.

1996 EUROPEAN CHAMPIONSHIP GROUP A FINAL TABLE

	P	W	D	L	GF	GA	P
England	3	2	1	0	7	2	7
Holland	3	1	1	1	3	4	4
Scotland	3	1	1	1	1	2	4
Switzerland	3	0	1	2	1	4	1

England drew Spain in the quarter-final showdown. The visitors, in a confident mood, were undeterred by the amazing support shown for the England side by the 75,000 crowd. England began the game in a positive fashion with chances for Neville, Gascoigne and Shearer bringing out the best in Zubizaretta in the Spanish goal. But, as the Spaniards settled, they began to show their class. Kiko had one 'goal' disallowed in the 22nd minute and then Salinas, a constant thorn in England's side, was also adjudged, this time wrongly, to be offside as he beat Seaman.

The second half was more one-sided as Spain created the better opportunities to win the match. However, 90 minutes of play could not separate the two sides and the game went into extra time. England's first exposure to the golden goal rule almost brought them dividends but Zubizaretta saved from Gascoigne. The two goalkeepers were both in outstanding form but, as the French referee blew for the end of extra time, only one could be the hero.

Spain buckled under the pressure of the penalty shoot-out, losing 4-2. Man of the Match Seaman saved from Hierro while Nadal missed the target as England progressed to the semi-finals. Three of England's successful penalty takers were Shearer, Platt and Gascoigne, the other was Pearce. The Nottingham Forest captain had spent six years carrying the burden of missing an England spot-kick in 1990 and now stepped forward to take his side's third kick with England already a goal to the good. His commitment to England's cause had never been questioned since he first pulled on an England shirt in 1987 – now he required every ounce of his courage as Wembley fell silent. Pearce ran up and, with a clean left-footed strike, buried the ball into the back of the Spanish net. The roar from the England crowd was as great as any other during the tournament – the chant of 'Psycho Psycho' reverberating around the stadium as Pearce exorcized his personal demon.

Spain's defeat was their first in 20 matches, but for England it meant progress to the semi-finals and a meeting with Germany. The hype surrounding England now reached stratospheric proportions. This was the sixth competitive game between England and Germany/West Germany

England played some outstanding football against the Dutch to win 4-1. Tony Adams, who had a good tournament, is seen here tackling his Arsenal team-mate Dennis Bergkamp.

since 1966 and England had failed to win any. Venables kept his squad focused on the job ahead and made one change to the side that began against Spain, bringing back Ince for Neville.

As at every England game thus far, the pre-match entertainment served to heighten the senses. England responded well. Ince hit a 25-yard drive, which Kopke tipped over the bar, and England's next attack resulted in a corner. Gascoigne chipped the ball in to the near post, Adams headed on and Shearer headed in. England 1 Germany 0, and only 87 minutes to go!

England's lead only lasted thirteen minutes as Kuntz levelled the scores. The sides swapped half-chances for the remainder of the first and second halves as the game, almost inevitably, stretched late into the evening. Extra time introduced the golden goal and opened up the game as nerve-ends jangled. McManaman was the first to carve an opening but he drove his shot too close to Kopke. Then Kuntz headed home only to see his

England move into the last eight of Euro '96 and make just one change for the game against Spain, Platt coming in for the suspended Ince. From left to right, back row: G. Neville, Platt, McManaman, Anderton, Seaman, Shearer. Front row: Gascoigne, Sheringham, Adams, Pearce, Southgate.

'goal' ruled out. The final opening was England's. Anderton found Shearer deep in the German box. England's number nine, spotting Gascoigne, played the ball across the face of the German goal. Alone, Gascoigne stretched every sinew in his body to reach the ball. Even the lightest of touches would have resulted in a goal but he was inches short. After 120 minutes nothing could separate these two sides and, as in 1990, the tie had to be decided by penalties.

As each of the statutory ten spotkicks were converted the tension grew to unbearable levels. Shearer, Platt, Pearce, Gascoigne and Sheringham all scored with confidence each celebrating in their own style (Pearce now with a discreet thumbs-up in marked contrast to just a few days earlier). England's sixth was taken by one of their up-and-coming stars, Gareth Southgate. He drove his shot too close to Kopke, who saved. Moller stepped up, converted his spot kick with confidence, and took his side into a final against the Czech Republic, who had beaten France on penalties in the other semi-final. Germany won the final on the golden goal rule.

For England, there was frustration but also pride. They had performed to the height of everyone's expectations and were unlucky not to progress to the final. For Venables, his spell in charge of the England team was all too short as he parted company with the FA following a dispute over an extension to his contract, which would have taken him through to the 1998 World Cup. He had been in charge for just 23 games: England had won 12 and lost only 2. He had introduced a system that suited the players at his disposal while their performances left English international football in much better health than he had found it.

top: David Seaman saves from Spain's Hierro in the penalty shoot-out.

middle: England get off to a flying start in the semi-final against Germany, Shearer heading home in the third minute.

bottom: Yet again in the semi-final of a major competition England lose to Germany. Gareth Southgate misses the vital spot kick and England are out: Sheringham and Ince move to console the taker.

ALAN SHEARER
Southampton/Blackburn Rovers/Newcastle United
Striker
63 international caps (1992-2000)

Technically Shearer is possibly the most complete striker that England have ever had. Apart from leading the line well using his upper body strength, he had tremendous power in both feet and was a fine header of the ball. First capped in 1992, he scored 30 goals in his 63 international games, a spell which was interrupted by injury. Following a successful Euro 2000 competition he retired, aged thirty, from the international scene.

DAVID SEAMAN
Queens Park Rangers/Arsenal
Goalkeeper
75 international caps (1988-2002)

Seaman was England's first choice goalkeeper in four major tournaments from Euro '96 to the World Cup of 2002. It was the first of those which made him a national hero, standing firm in goal and stopping one of Spain's penalty kicks in the quarter final shoot out. A great shot stopper, Seaman at his best pulled off a number of amazing saves in the England jersey, which sometimes, like in the 5-1 victory in Germany, changed the course of the game. Although he took the blame for Brazil's freak goal that beat England in the 2002 World Cup, his overall record cements his place in the England Hall of Fame.

FOREVER
ENGLAND

CHAPTER**NINE**

FOREVER ENGLAND 1996-2004

Glenn Hoddle, a gifted player whose international appearances spanned the period 1980 to 1988. His successful period in charge of Chelsea had put him in the frame for the England job.

Glenn Hoddle replaced Terry Venables as England manager after the European Championships and set about qualifying for the 1998 World Cup. In England's group were two nations, Moldova and Georgia, whom England had never played before. The group also included Poland, whom England now faced for an incredible fourth time in World Cup qualification, and the Italians, whom England had beaten just once in five competitive games.

Hoddle became the ninth England manager and the fifth to have played for the national side. An England career spanning eight years should have accrued more caps for Hoddle than the 53 he did receive but both the managers he played under, Greenwood and Robson, were apparently unwilling to build a team around probably the most gifted England player of the time. His brief managerial career had seen him revitalize first Swindon Town then Chelsea.

There was no opportunity for the new manager to ease his way into the England hotseat: his first four games in charge were all World Cup qualifiers. Hoddle selected largely from the Euro '96 squad, adding Manchester United's rising star David Beckham for his first taste of international football and bringing Southampton's Matt Le Tissier back from the international wilderness.

There was no place in the Hoddle set-up for David Platt, who had inherited Bryan Robson's role at the heart of England's midfield in the 1990 World Cup. His trademark late runs into the box helped him to amass 27 goals for England in 62 games, a very creditable return considering the number of times he featured only as a substitute.

England's first match under Hoddle was away to Moldova and could have been a disaster for the new manager but, with goals from Nick Barmby, Paul Gascoigne and Alan Shearer, England's qualification campaign was on its way with a 3-0 win. Then Shearer netted both goals in a 2-0 win over Poland while Teddy Sheringham and Les Ferdinand got the goals in a 2-0 win in Georgia. Next came Italy's visit to Wembley.

Tottenham's goalkeeper, Ian Walker, came in for David Seaman while Hoddle picked Southampton's Matthew Le Tissier to start the match. However, all did not go according to plan. Chelsea's Zola put Italy ahead after 18 minutes. Le Tissier was unable to impose himself on the game and was substituted on the hour, and England were unable to break down the visitors and suffered a first defeat under the new manager.

These World Cup games were followed by two friendlies in May 1997, both wins, over Mexico and South Africa. England breezed through their next three qualifiers, 2-0 against Georgia and the same against Poland before putting four past Moldova. Italy dropped two points in draws with Poland and Georgia, which opened the door for England. The final group match, in Rome, would decide who would qualify automatically and who would have to chance their arm via the play-offs.

In the summer of 1997, England went to France to play in a four-team tournament as preparation for the finals. They dealt a psychological blow to the Italians with a 2-0 win thanks to goals from Ian Wright and Paul Scholes. They then, luckily, beat the hosts 1-0 thanks to a Shearer goal. With Brazil drawing their other two games, England went into their last match knowing victory in the Tournoi de France was theirs. England lost the game 1-0, but won the trophy. The Italian game at the Tournoi also saw the passing of another England great. After 76 games, Stewart Pearce, best remembered for one penalty missed and another scored for his country, had played for the last time in England's defence.

The showdown in Rome was not a classic game but it was nail-biting for all concerned. Italy had to win, England needed only the draw.

Hoddle on the training ground with rising star David Beckham.

England's record in Italy was not good – they had lost every game since 1961. But, unlike at Wembley, Hoddle got his tactics right and his side kept the Italians at bay turning in an heroic performance in a 0-0 draw. England were through to the World Cup, Italy would have to qualify via the play-offs.

Ian Wright is brought down by Italy's Cannavaro during the crucial qualifying tie for the 1998 World Cup. The point from the 0-0 draw was enough to give England top position in their group.

England's World Cup team for their opening match versus Tunisia. From left to right, back row: Ince, Campbell, Adams, Anderton, Seaman, Southgate. Front row: Sheringham, Batty, Le Saux, Scholes, Shearer.

1998 WORLD CUP QUALIFYING GROUP TWO FINAL TABLE

	P	W	D	L	GF	GA	P
England	8	6	1	1	15	2	19
Italy	8	5	3	0	11	1	18
Poland	8	3	1	4	10	12	10
Georgia	8	3	1	4	7	9	10
Moldova	8	0	0	8	2	21	0

Hoddle now had seven games to build on a very successful qualification campaign and realize the nation's dream of World Cup success. The first, against Cameroon, resulted in a 2-0 win. However, three months later, England were put to the sword by a Chilean side inspired by a truly world-class player, Salas, who scored both the visitors' goals. A 1-1 draw with Switzerland followed before an emphatic 3-0 win over Portugal. Three less inspiring games followed and Hoddle announced his squad.

There was no place for Gascoigne. A true footballing genius and in his prime one of the world's best players, injury and controversy littered his career, limiting his international performances to 57 in nine years. His most memorable moment? The goal against Scotland in Euro '96, one of the best ever scored by an Englishman, would always represent the best of Gascoigne.

The World Cup was well underway by the time England took to the field in their first game, against Tunisia. The England manager chose to leave out Beckham and Liverpool's Michael Owen, favourites of the fans and journalists alike, preferring the experience offered by Teddy Sheringham and Darren Anderton.

England took some while to get into their stride and had to wait until the 28th minute for their first clear-cut chance, when Graeme Le Saux set up Paul Scholes, whose effort was saved well by El

Quaer in the Tunisian goal. Minutes later, El Quaer stopped a Sheringham volley before Shearer headed home a Le Saux free-kick with half-time rapidly approaching.

After the break, England again had the pick of the chances while Seaman was spared any real test. As the game was drifting to a finish, England's army of fans was rewarded with the sight of Owen about to make his entrance as the third youngest player ever to appear in the World Cup finals. Replacing Sheringham, Owen made a couple of darting runs to whet the appetite of England's fans, but it was Scholes who was to have the last word with an arcing shot from the edge of the penalty box to secure a very comfortable and enjoyable 2-0 win for his country.

England then took on Romania in Toulouse. Again the pre-match speculation was about whether Hoddle would play Owen and Beckham. Again Hoddle resisted the temptation and began the game with the same side that had beat the Tunisians, save for the replacement of the injured Gareth Southgate with Gary Neville. Romania presented England with different problems than had the Africans and tested Seaman from long range whenever possible. The closest they came was after 27 minutes when Ilie's chip rebounded off the England crossbar. Minutes later, Ince left the field with an ankle injury to be replaced by Beckham. Suddenly, the noise from England's supporters went up a notch or two, as did the team's application with some nice touches from the Manchester United man, while a good opening from Scholes went begging.

England came out for the second half looking to build on the positives but were stunned within two minutes when Moldovan put the Romanians

ahead from close range. Far from sitting back on their lead, Romania pressed for the killer goal. Hoddle again replaced Sheringham with Owen. Owen's pace immediately had the Romanians defending deeper. With just seven minutes of the game remaining, Owen fired home the equalizer and England's travelling army went delirious. England had seemed to have saved the day and were settling for a hard-earned draw when Chelsea's Dan Petrescu stole in behind the England defence to slot home the winner through Seaman's legs. Owen was denied a second equalizer in added time by the thickness of a post.

England travelled north to Lens for their final group match, against Colombia. The fans got what they wanted in the inclusion of Owen and Beckham from the start. They also witnessed a fine performance, which had some commentators tipping England as possible champions. England fashioned a number of good chances in the opening 15 minutes as Scholes, Owen and Le Saux all went close but it was the impressive Anderton who was to break to deadlock with a stunning drive from a tight angle to give his side the lead. A second came on the half hour. Preciado fouled Paul Ince on the edge of the Colombian penalty box. Up stepped Beckham, whose kick flew over the wall and buried itself in the back of the net.

Colombia introduced three fresh players for the second half. But it was Hoddle's side that fashioned a number of chances, the highlight being a mesmerizing run by defender Sol Campbell, but the third goal did not materialize; England settled for 2-0 and a place in the knock-out phase.

1998 WORLD CUP
GROUP G FINAL TABLE

	P	W	D	L	GF	GA	P
Romania	3	2	1	0	4	2	7
England	3	2	0	1	5	2	6
Colombia	3	1	0	2	1	3	3
Tunisia	3	0	1	2	1	4	1

England's second place in Group G meant a second- round draw against one of the group winners, Argentina. With Gary Neville now preferred to a fit-again Southgate, Hoddle named the same XI that had beaten Colombia:

> Seaman (Arsenal), Neville (Manchester United), Adams (Arsenal), Campbell (Tottenham Hotspur), Anderton (Tottenham Hotspur), Beckham (Manchester United), Ince (Liverepool), Le Saux (Chelsea), Scholes (Manchester United), Owen (Liverpool), Shearer (Newcastle United).

The game, staged in St Etienne, was just five minutes old when Seaman was adjudged to have pulled down Batistuta. The Argentine hero picked himself up from the ground to slot home the first goal of the game from the penalty spot. England responded with the game's second dubious penalty as Owen went down for Shearer to convert.

There was no let up in the excitement as, on 16 minutes, Beckham played a through ball to Owen on halfway. The Liverpool player turned his man and set off, at a blistering pace, for the Argentine goal. Entering his opponents' penalty box, Owen appeared to have pushed himself too wide but angled a shot to leave Roa standing and send the England faithful into raptures: 2-1 to England.

Ince and Scholes both had chances that would have put England out of sight before Zanetti equalized with the seconds ticking down to the break.

The first half had exceeded everyone's expectations and both sides came out unchanged for the second half. Within a minute, the action continued, decisively. Simeone barged Beckham to the floor, a clear free kick. But, while the England player was grounded he raised a leg, which connected with the Argentine who theatrically fell. The incident took place right in front of the Danish referee, Mr Nielson, who instantly took out his red card and showed it to the England man. One second of madness not only robbed England of a key player for the rest of the game but was also a setback which Beckham would be reminded of, not least by opposing fans at English club grounds, for years.

Following Beckham's departure, Hoddle regrouped his side who went on to produce an heroic performance. Tony Adams marshalled the defence in one of the Arsenal captain's best-ever performances for England. Shearer ran tirelessly. Paul Merson and Southgate came on for Scholes and Le Saux as the game entered the last quarter. With just nine minutes remaining, England thought they had snatched victory as Campbell rose to head home in a crowded penalty area. As the England players celebrated, the Argentines responded to the referee's decision of a foul by Shearer on Roa and almost created a goal-scoring opportunity of their own with England's defence in disarray.

Extra time brought chances for both sides but there was no golden goal and the game ended in a 2-2 draw and would now be decided on a

Sol Campbell mixes it with Marian Hristov during the 0-0 draw with Bulgaria in October 1998.

penalty shoot-out. Argentina's Berti converted the first while Shearer responded: 1-1. Crespo then missed and Ince had the chance to put England into a lead, he failed and the scores remained 1-1. Veron and Merson both scored, then Gallardo and Owen to make the score 3-3. Ayala put his side ahead: 4-3. The pressure was now on David Batty, England's final penalty taker. The Leeds United midfielder had never taken a penalty kick for his club but now had to score to keep his country in the World Cup. He didn't and England were eliminated from a major tournament on penalties for the third time inside a decade.

England v. Argentina was judged by many as the match of the tournament. It was surpassed for some by the Argentines' quarter-final against Holland, which was won in the 90th minute by the Dutch. Brazil then beat the Dutch in one semi-final while France beat Croatia in the other. Following this, Brazil put in a strangely lethargic performance in the final itself, losing 3-0 to the hosts – who became world champions for the first time.

England's Euro 2000 qualifiers began in Stockholm. When Shearer put England ahead with a rasping drive after less than two minutes of the game, their confidence soared. But, from that moment on, England's attempt at qualification was

England need all the points and goals they can get as they try to qualify for the Euro 2000 finals. The 6-0 win over Luxembourg at Wembley was helped by a fine performance from Michael Owen.

The fans' and players' favourite – and an England hero on the field during his playing career – Kevin Keegan was invited to fill the shoes of the controversy-prone Hoddle in February 1999.

to be a roller-coaster ride. Eight largely disappointing group games were to be followed, luckily, by a home-and-away play-off against the Scots. If that were not enough, the manager's hotseat was to be occupied by three different men. Sweden turned round the game in Stockholm, winning 2-1. That was a disappointing outcome but England's next game, at home to Bulgaria, proved almost as bad as the game ended in a 0-0 draw.

England did then win, 3-0 in Luxembourg but, as the group games took their winter break, England were in third place. The performance of the team in the qualifying matches mirrored a disquiet in the England camp since the World Cup and the publication of the manager's account of the tournament. Hoddle then scored a personal own-goal with public comments about reincarnation. Add to this his apparent reliance on a faith-healer and it was clear that the manager's days were numbered. With the pressure mounting, Hoddle stepped down in

February 1999. Although only in charge for 28 games, Hoddle's record of 17 wins, 4 draws and 7 defeats left him with a win ratio on a par with Ramsey.

The FA installed Howard Wilkinson as acting manager for the visit of world champions, France. England were well beaten 2-0 and any real chance Wilkinson had of being given the job on a permanent basis following England's poor display disappeared.

The job was given to the people's choice, Kevin Keegan, whose managerial career had seen him revive Newcastle United and Fulham. Keegan was given little more than a 50/50 chance of getting England to Euro 2000, either as winners of the group or through the play-offs but his presence appeared to breath new life into England's campaign as they defeated Poland 3-0 at Wembley thanks to a Scholes hat-trick.

However, when his side failed to beat runaway group leaders Sweden at Wembley, talk turned to

Paul Scholes scores a brilliant hat-trick for England as they defeat Poland 3-0 at Wembley in March 1999.

2000 EUROPEAN CHAMPIONSHIPS
QUALIFYING GROUP FIVE FINAL TABLE

	P	W	D	L	GF	GA	P
Sweden	8	7	1	0	10	1	22
England	8	3	4	1	14	4	13
Poland	8	4	1	3	12	8	13
Bulgaria	8	2	2	4	6	8	8
L'bourg	8	0	0	8	2	23	0

England drew Scotland. The tension among the fans and the hype in the media grew to unimaginable heights as the days counted down. The first leg was to be played at Hampden Park, in front of over 50,000 partisan Scots. In the opening minutes, the Scots had the better of the chances as the home team went in search of the first goal. But England weathered the early storm. The influential Gallacher was booked for a foul on Owen, which meant he would miss the second game, and then England struck. Scholes made a darting run into the Scotland penalty box from a Campbell chip and hammered the ball home past a despairing Sullivan. Hampden Park fell silent.

The Scots lifted themselves immediately and almost levelled the scores through Gallacher, but his shot was well blocked by Seaman. Scotland continued to press, having two penalty claims turned down by the Spanish referee, but then succumbed to England just minutes before the break. A Beckham free-kick was headed home by Scholes, whose celebration earned him a yellow card. The second half had little of the drama of the first with England comfortably in control and looking the only team likely to score. At the final whistle, with an emptying Hampden Park echoing to the boos of the home fans, England looked home and dry.

preparation for the World Cup in 2002 rather than the impending European Championships. England drew their final game, in Poland, and now held their breath as Sweden entertained Poland knowing that anything but a win for Sweden would spell England's exit; Poland needed a point to qualify for the play-offs at England's expense. However, Sweden won 2-0 and England were through to the play-offs.

Wembley was packed for the return match and the Scots played, as so many of their predecessors had before them, with passion, pride and a willingness to die for the cause. England turned in a dire performance. Only courageous defending and world-class goalkeeping from Seaman restricted the Scots to an agonizing one goal. The closeness of the scoreline kept the game bubbling until the final whistle.

In the run-up to the finals, England played two South American giants, starting with Argentina. Without posing a serious threat to the visitors, England performed with credit in a 0-0 draw. The performance of Emile Heskey of Leicester City was the highlight of the evening for Keegan. However, the game was overshadowed by news on the morning of the game of the death of Stanley Matthews. Eighty-five years old on his death, Matthews's career had been remarkable for its longevity. He had played for England at the age of forty-two, winning the last of his 54 caps in 1957. And as the tributes rolled in from around the world, one theme emerged above all others: one of England's all-time greats, Matthews was also a true gentleman, always modest about his own incomparable talents and quick to praise others.

Brazil were the next visitors to Wembley. Owen, who had had a stop-and-start season due to a recurring hamstring injury, boosted his own and England's self-confidence with a fine goal, using his speed of movement inside the area to create a shooting opportunity which he duly scored from. Brazil equalized thanks to a lack of concentration in the England defence as the seconds ticked down to half-time. With no goals in the second half, the game ended 1-1 with most commentators and fans pleased with the home team's performance.

A shot from the crunch play-off match at Wembley for a place at Euro 2000. England's strong-running Emile Heskey is tussling with John Collins as Scotland battle for survival.

England's final game at Wembley before Euro 2000 was against the Ukraine, the best side not to have qualified for the finals. Robbie Fowler poached a first goal from two yards while the second came via the most unexpected route – the boot of Tony Adams. England's final game before the finals saw the team fly to Malta to commemorate the island's Football Association's 100th anniversary. A bizarre game ended in a 2-1 win for England, but not before England's debutant goalkeeper, Ipswich Town's Richard Wright, had conceded two penalties, saving one and being credited with the Maltese goal as the spot kick struck an upright and rebounded into the net off Wright's head. The game also holds a dubious record as the islanders substituted every one of their players during the course of the match so that each member of their squad would gain a full cap in this historic encounter.

Paul Ince gets to the ball ahead of Silvinho during England's match with Brazil in May 2000, which ended in a 1-1 draw at Wembley.

England's Group A opponents in the championships were Germany, Romania and Portugal. Only against Portugal had England enjoyed any tournament success in recent years, but this Portuguese side was the best since their team of the mid-1960s. With an attacking midfield comprising Figo and Rui Costa, they were one of the dark horses of the competition.

In his team selection, Keegan plumped for experience, selecting nine of the players who had started the World Cup match against Argentina two years previously:

Seaman (Arsenal), P. Neville (Manchester United), Campbell (Tottenham Hotspur), Adams (Arsenal), G. Neville (Manchester United), Ince (Middlesbrough), Beckham (Manchester United), Scholes (Manchester United), Shearer (Newcastle United), Owen (Liverpool), McManaman (Real Madrid).

In just the third minute, Beckham delivered an inch-perfect cross from the right touchline for Scholes to head home, courtesy of the underside of the bar. The Portuguese had ear-marked

A wonder start for England at Euro 2000 as Paul Scholes heads home in the third minute of the first match against Portugal.

England's team against Germany. From left to right, back row: Wise, Keown, Campbell, Ince, Seaman, Shearer. Front row: Scholes, Owen, Beckham, P. Neville, G. Neville.

Scholes and his trademark late runs into the box as a major threat and, on England's first attack, they had fallen for it. Despite one or two close calls, England were able to double their lead before the game was a quarter of the way through when Beckham provided the cross for an unmarked McManaman to half-volley into the roof of the net.

At 2-0, the travelling England army had plenty to cheer, but Portugal were not going to lie down. Figo hit an amazing shot from almost 30 yards into the top corner of England's net. The goal galvanized the Portuguese, stringing together moves that pulled England's defenders one way, then the other. One such move created an opening for a cross to the near post. Joao Pinto swooped and guided a header past Seaman to level the scores.

The second half began with Heskey replacing the injured Owen. England were beginning to dominate more of the game. However, on the

hour, Portugal broke and took the lead as Gomes scored. England, particularly Scholes, had half-chances to level the score but the game drifted away from an increasingly despondent side who had, in the cold light of day, looked second best. The final whistle almost came as a relief to the first England side to let a two-goal lead slip to lose in a major finals since the 1970 World Cup.

Constant attention surrounded both the England and German camps in the days leading up to their game and both sides lost players to injury: Adams and McManaman for England and Bierhoff for Germany.

England fans outnumbered Germans inside the Charleroi stadium by three to one and outsang their opponents throughout the 90 minutes. The game itself began tentatively. The Germans had a couple of free-kicks around the England box but Seaman remained well-protected. England took their time to get into the game then, in the final fifteen minutes of the first half, created two goal-scoring

Alan Shearer heads England's winning goal over Germany.

opportunities. Owen, connecting with a Philip Neville cross, rose above the German defence placing a firm header which Khan pushed onto his own post. Then Beckham provided the incisive ball of the half for Scholes who drove his shot at the German goalkeeper.

England began the second half as they had ended the first, just about edging the contest. Then, on 53 minutes, Beckham was fouled ten yards inside the German half. Picking himself up off the ground, Beckham looped the free-kick into the German area. The curve on the ball caused four defenders, Scholes and Owen to miss the ball. However, Shearer was waiting, unmarked, seven yards from goal. He stooped and placed a firm header out of Khan's reach and into the German net. Wheeling away with his trademark celebration of the raised right hand, England's captain had given his side a priceless lead.

The Germans upped the pace but England had learnt from their experiences against Portugal and allowed the German side, for whom Jancker remained a constant threat, little room to create an opening. Scholl dragged a shot across Seaman's goal. Then from a corner Seaman saved a scuffed shot on the line only to set up Jancker with a glorious chance to level the scores from eight yards. He drove his shot hard enough but just wide of the goal.

The minutes ticked by agonizingly slowly. One of Liverpool's young stars, Steven Gerrard, replaced another, Owen, while Nicky Barmby

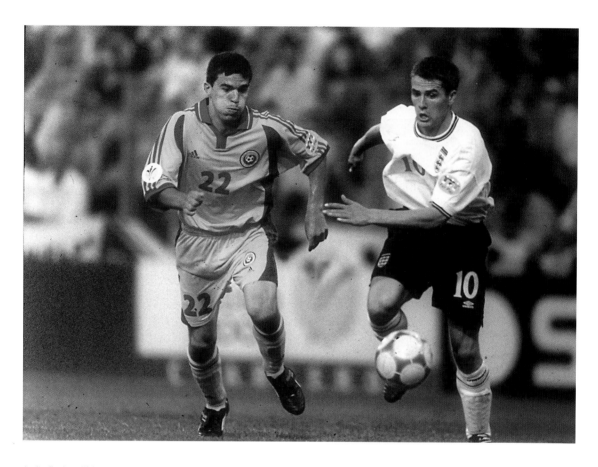

In the final qualifying game, Michael Owen breaks away from Romania's Cosmin Contra and scores his first goal of the tournament.

came on for a limping Scholes. Throughout, England remained firm at the back with nothing getting past Campbell and Keown. Germany's chances began to dry up as the noise from the England fans grew louder and louder. On the final whistle the England team and fans celebrated as if they had won the competition. England's side in the early stages of the game had appeared weighed down by the expectation, now they looked on top of the world: England 1 Germany 0.

England's pride was short-lived. The behaviour of some of the team's fans before and after the match had been as bad as any in the depressingly long history of violence surrounding England. Within twenty-four hours of the side's historic win, UEFA was threatening England with expulsion from the competition if there were to be a repeat. Keegan's task was to secure one point from their final game in the knowledge that England had not beaten Romania since 1970.

England emerged from the tunnel with a surprise in store for their fans, Seaman had sustained a late injury and was replaced by Nigel Martyn of Leeds United. Apart from that one

THE LAST EVER MATCH BENEATH THE TWIN TOWERS

Nationwide
THE ENGLAND TEAM SPONSOR

FIFA WORLD CUP 2002 QUALIFIER – GROUP 9

ENGLAND v **GERMANY**

Wembley · Saturday 7th October 2000 · Kick off 3.00 pm

After seventy-seven years of sporting history, Wembley Stadium hosts its final association football match. The programme cover gives recognition to the last game beneath the Twin Towers.

change, England fielded the same side that had beaten the Germans.

As early as the second minute, Martyn produced a world-class save to keep out Ille's blistering free-kick. It gave the England goalkeeper a huge boost of confidence but served as a sign of the night ahead for England's fans. After 21 minutes Romania took the lead as Chivu's chip to the far post left Martyn stranded. The Romanians had opportunities to increase their lead but, with less than five minutes remaining of the first half, England hit back. First, Ince drove into the

Romanian box to be pulled down for a penalty. Shearer sent the goalkeeper the wrong way to level the scores. Then, on the stroke of half-time, Owen sprung the Romanian offside trap to claim his first goal of the finals. England were 2-1 up, totally against the run of play.

Keegan demanded that his players consolidate their position in the opening spell of the second half but, following a defensive mix-up, Martyn failed to properly clear a cross to allow Munteanu to drive home the equalizer. Although the impetus was now with Romania again, England looked to be holding on comfortably for a 2-2 draw as the minutes ticked away. Then, with the quarter-finals in sight, England's stand-in left-back, Phil Neville, brought down Moldovan with a clumsy challenge inside his own box. Ganea scored from the resulting penalty and England were out of the tournament.

2000 EUROPEAN CHAMPIONSHIPS
GROUP A FINAL TABLE

	P	W	D	L	GF	GA	P
Portugal	3	3	0	0	7	2	9
Romania	3	1	1	1	4	4	4
England	3	1	0	2	3	6	3
Germany	3	0	1	2	1	5	1

As the result sank in, the attention focussed on those players for whom this might be their England swansong. Shearer had announced before the tournament that he would be retiring from the international scene. He had more than justified his place in the side during Euro 2000 and, with 30 goals in 63 games for England, would undoubtedly be a very tough act to follow.

Other changes would be down to the manager as press and fans called for youth. Would this be the end for Seaman, Ince and Adams?

France won the tournament to add the European Championships to the World Cup title they had won two years before. In the final they defeated Italy 2-1, thanks to a golden goal in extra time. Following their summer break, England went to Paris to play the all-conquering French. Few gave Keegan's team much hope yet, thanks to an Owen goal, England emerged with a creditable 1-1 draw. World Cup qualifiers now loomed. England had been drawn against Germany, Finland, Greece and Albania in what was generally considered to be one of the weaker European groups.

England's first game was against Germany, the last match to be played at Wembley before the stadium's demolition. Germany dominated much of the clash. They took the lead midway through the first half thanks to a thirty-yard free-kick from Liverpool's Dietmar Hamann and never looked like relinquishing it. Adams and Beckham had England's best chances, but, at the final whistle, the boos rang out around the old stadium.

The England camp was then thrown into turmoil as Keegan resigned while the fans were

Sven-Goran Eriksson was the Football Association's choice as manager to succeed Kevin Keegan It was a controversial but bold decision and he became the first foreign national to run the England side.

still making their way home from the most disappointing of Wembley occasions. There was a second qualifier just days away, in Finland, and the FA quickly moved to install Howard Wilkinson as coach for the game. On a bumpy pitch and against a side eager to add to England's woes, Wilkinson's team put in a battling performance and, but for two dubious refereeing decisions, would have taken the three points.

A few weeks after that disappointing 0-0 result, the FA announced its decision regarding Keegan's replacement. In a dramatic break with tradition the position was awarded to Sven-Goran Eriksson,

the manager of Rome giants Lazio, who became England's first ever foreign coach.

But before the new man took charge, Peter Taylor was installed as England's temporary manager for one game, in Italy. England lost that game 1-0, but Taylor did make a few England watchers sit up and take interest as he made David Beckham the team's captain.

The Swede's first game in charge was a friendly against Spain which England won 3-0, again with Beckham leading the team.

England's World Cup bid, however, was in crisis as Eriksson took charge. Then, with two wins in two

Steven Gerrard, one of a number of young England players who has come through and one who will be an automatic selection for the next few years.

games, first at home to Finland, where the new captain scored the winner, and then away to Albania, there was now an outside chance of the team making the finals.

A 4-0 win over Mexico was followed by another World Cup away win, this time 2-0 in Greece, which gave England real hope of qualification with three games remaining. The first of them was the return match in Germany.

A packed Olympic Stadium in Munich saw the home side take the lead in just the sixth minute. Owen equalised for England and then Gerrard rifled England into a half-time lead against the run of play. The second half had England's travelling fans pinching themselves in disbelief and elevated Eriksson to god-like status in his adopted homeland. Within three minutes of the restart Owen made it 3-1, and then on 66 minutes the Liverpool forward completed a remarkable hat-trick. His club colleague, Heskey, then added a fifth. The final 5-1 scoreline was England's best in World Cup qualification against a major side, possibly England's best away result of all time and Germany's worst home defeat in living memory.

A lacklustre 2-0 win at home to Albania followed the fireworks of Munich, but England were now in the driving seat for automatic qualification. They needed just a draw from their final game at Old Trafford against Greece. It turned out, however, to be anything but a stroll in the park. Twice England found themselves behind. Then, as the game entered added time with England 2-1 down, the home side won a free-kick 25 yards out, central to the Greek goal. It was their last chance. Beckham, who had played out of his skin for 90 minutes, stepped up and buried the ball in the back of the net. England's topsy-turvy qualification programme ended on the most dramatic high possible and Beckham secured his place in England's all-time dream team.

2002 WORLD CUP QUALIFYING GROUP NINE FINAL TABLE

	P	W	D	L	GF	GA	P
England	8	5	2	1	16	6	17
Germany	8	5	2	1	14	10	17
Finland	8	3	3	2	12	7	12
Greece	8	2	1	5	7	17	7
Albania	8	1	0	7	5	14	3

Eriksson had six games before the World Cup finals began for England in Japan, who were co-hosting the tournament with South Korea. He experimented with players and formations in all of them, while drawing four, winning one and losing one. The 2002 finals were unique in many ways, not least because one man, David Beckham, was more popular with the home fans than any other player and most teams, including England. So, when Beckham sustained a major injury in a Champions League tie, breaking his metatarsal, there was as much concern in Tokyo as in London. When Gary Neville sustained a similar injury, which forced him to withdraw from the squad, the fans in the Far East were less concerned, but England's chances of progressing beyond the group stages were starting to be viewed as slim.

Eriksson could not envisage playing without Beckham and selected him, even though he was barely half fit, for the first of England's group matches, against Sweden. It proved to be a dour match, Sol Campbell scoring England's goal from a

A flying header from Sol Campbell gives England an early goal in their opening World Cup 2002 game. Sweden's Allback, Hedman and Melberg fail to intercept.

header in the first half only for Sweden to gain a draw in the second.

The England captain had only played for an hour against Sweden, but he was determined not to miss his side's second group match, in Sapporo, against Argentina.

The England line-up was as follows:

Seaman (Arsenal), Mills (Leeds United), Cole (Arsenal), Ferdinand (Leeds United), Campbell (Arsenal), Beckham (Manchester United), Butt (Manchester United), Scholes (Manchester United), Hargreaves (Bayern Munich), Heskey (Liverpool), Owen (Liverpool).

Five of the XI had suffered defeat at the hands of Argentina four years previously and from the kick-off there was a determination among the team not to suffer a repeat. There was a tense opening to the game and in the first half hour Argentina were looking the better side, but only just. Then as both managers were preparing their half-time team talks, Owen burst into the Argentine penalty area and was brought down by Pochettino. This was Beckham's moment. Like Stuart Pearce at Euro '96, Beckham just had to score. He ran up and hit the ball hard and low down the centre of the goal. Cavallero had chosen to dive and stood no chance, 1-0 to England.

The second period saw England take greater control of the game and create the better chances, the best of them from Sheringham, who had replaced Heskey, and Scholes – either of which could have secured the points. However, Aimar always looked dangerous and kept the England defence on its toes right to the end. But in the end, the single goal proved decisive and all but secured a place in the next stage for Eriksson's men. The Swede had now masterminded wins over Germany and Argentina, could he take England all the way?

The final group game saw England draw 0-0 in the searing afternoon heat against Nigeria. It was not an ideal result, but one which England increasingly played for as the game went on. Qualification from what had been dubbed the 'Group of Death' was secured and England could stay at the World Cup party, unlike Argentina, France and Portugal.

David Beckham peels away after scoring (from the penalty spot) the goal that turned out to be the winner against Argentina. Sinclair joins the celebrations.

2002 WORLD CUP GROUP F FINAL TABLE

	P	W	D	L	GF	GA	P
Sweden	3	1	2	0	4	3	5
England	3	1	2	0	2	1	5
Argentina	3	1	1	1	2	2	4
Nigeria	3	0	1	2	1	3	1

After defeating Denmark in the second round this England team faced Brazil for a place in the 2002 World Cup semi-final. From left to right, back row: Owen, Campbell, Heskey, Mills, Seaman, Ferdinand. Front row: Butt, A. Cole, Beckham (captain), Scholes, Sinclair.

England drew Denmark for their second phase game and had a dream start. Beckham's fifth minute corner was met by Rio Ferdinand. Sorensen made a hash of protecting his goal and the ball crossed the line to give England the lead. (Although clearly an own-goal, FIFA credited it to Ferdinand.) England's lead was doubled on 22 minutes as Sinclair and Butt combined to allow Owen to poach his first of the tournament. When Heskey latched onto a dangerous ball from Beckham, burying his first-time shot into the back of the Denmark net, the game was all but over with the second half yet to play. Eriksson's side cruised through the second period and now looked forward to a quarter-final showdown with tournament favourites Brazil.

England v. Brazil captured the imagination of the Japanese public as it pitted their two favourite foreign teams against each other. Despite an early free-kick from Ronaldinho, England settled well. Then, on 23 minutes, a long speculative ball from Heskey into the heart of the Brazilian defence was not controlled well by Lucio. Owen saw his chance, stole the ball from the defender and, deceiving Marcos in the Brazilian goal with the slightest of feints, calmly planted the ball into the net. The attention now switched to Beckham. The England's captain's fitness had improved with every game but he was still far from his best. Just

after the goal, he had to leave the field for treatment. He returned, creating a double-chance for himself.

The game was approaching half time when Seaman fell awkwardly, requiring lengthy attention. It was this added time that gave Brazil the chance to forge one last opening. Ronaldinho's mazy run created an opening for Rivaldo whose classy finish brought the scores level. This seemed the turning-point in the game. Brazil came out for the second half looking the more likely. Their second goal, from Ronaldinho, direct from a free-kick 35 yards from the England goal, appeared to be more of a misplaced cross than a shot. Either way, within 13 minutes of play England had gone from being 1-0 up to 2-1 down.

The drama continued, as Ronaldinho's high tackle on Mills earned him a harsh straight red card. Was this the luck that England needed to get back into the game, with still a half hour left to play? The answer was a conclusive 'no'. England spent the remainder of the match chasing shadows. They could barely get hold of the ball let alone mount a concerted assault on the Brazilian goal. At the end, the disappointment of England's second-half performance was clear: they had got a great chance, they blew it and everyone could see that they had.

For the first time, the management of Eriksson was called into question. Luckily for him losing to Brazil has never been seen as a disgrace although, with the world's favourite team down to ten men, England may have to wait a long time to get a better chance to see them off in such an important fixture. Brazil went on to win the World Cup with goals from Ronaldo dispatching Turkey in their semi-final and Germany, 2-0, in the final.

The Euro 2004 qualification programme was soon under way. After a 1-1 draw in a friendly against the tournament's future hosts, Portugal, England scraped a 2-1 win in Slovakia and then were even more fortunate to gain a 2-2 draw against Macedonia at Southampton's St Mary's ground. Despite gaining four points from two games, the campaign had not got off to the best of starts.

An embarrassing 1-3 defeat to Australia was followed by just a 2-0 win over Euro 2004 minnows Liechtenstein. The fans and the press were not amused. Eriksson and his side had only a few days to turn things around as Turkey, World Cup semi-finalists and group leaders, came to town.

Under great pressure, England delivered a fine performance, probably the best at a home venue since Euro '96. They dominated much of the game and deservedly took the lead on 76 minutes through substitute Darius Vassell. Beckham converted a penalty in the second minute of injury time to secure the points, but the 2-0 scoreline didn't flatter the home side.

Slovakia were England's final opponents of the 2002/03 season and, as in the first game in

Born in Canada and playing in Germany with Bayern Munich, Owen Hargreaves could have chosen to play for Wales, Germany, Canada or England. England believe he made the right choice!

The Turkey v. England game raised high emotions in both camps. England's team for the decider was, from left to right, back row: Terry, Heskey, James, Rooney, Butt, Campbell. Front row: Scholes, Gerrard, Beckham, Neville, Cole.

Bratislava, they took the lead. However, England again turned the score round and thanks to a brace from Owen secured the three points with a 2-1 win. More importantly, with three games to go England's young side were now in the driving seat to qualify automatically for Euro 2004.

Sven's team completed another turnaround in Skopje against Macedonia. At 1-0 down, Heskey came on to change the game in England's favour

setting up Everton's seventeen-year-old Wayne Rooney for his first international goal and setting England on their way to a 2-1 win. A second win against Liechtenstein set up a critical decider against Turkey in Istanbul with England needing a draw to qualify automatically. They did so, dominating the game and even having the luxury of Beckham missing a penalty. The game ended 0-0 and England topped the group.

2004 EUROPEAN CHAMPIONSHIPS
QUALIFYING GROUP SEVEN FINAL TABLE

	Pd	Wn	Dn	Ls	GF	GA	Ps
England	8	6	2	0	14	5	20
Turkey	8	6	1	1	17	5	19
Slovakia	8	3	1	4	11	9	10
Macedonia	8	1	3	4	11	14	6
Liechten.	8	0	1	7	2	22	1

Turkey 0 England 0, the final game covered in this book, mirrors the first official game, Scotland 0 England 0, in that is was a goalless draw away from home against an opponent desperate to beat the Three Lions. As with the first game and nearly

all those played by England since, the recording of the result hides much about the football match as an event, as something which focuses the attention of the nation. The pre-match build-up to the game in Istanbul elevated a game of football to the front pages and TV news programmes with concerns over potential crowd trouble, the England team's safety and preparation. This was on top of perennial troubles surrounding team selection, injuries, the club-versus-country argument and the future of the manager. On this occasion there was also the possibility of an England team strike over Rio Ferdinand's drugs testing. During the game, there was a brawl between both sets of players in the tunnel at half-time, which resulted in fines for both teams. The fall-out of the game also led Aston Villa to cancel the contract of Alpay, the Turkish player who had goaded Beckham during the game. Despite all this, England had produced a fine controlled performance and won the group ahead of Turkey.

Eriksson's record now looked mightily impressive: just one defeat in 19 competitive games, to Brazil at the World Cup. Best of all, England now had a crop of world-class players willing to battle for the cause: Beckham, Owen, Hargreaves, Campbell, Gerrard, Scholes and rising stars such as Rooney and Joe Cole who would be leading the charge for years to come, starting with the Euro 2004 finals in Portugal.

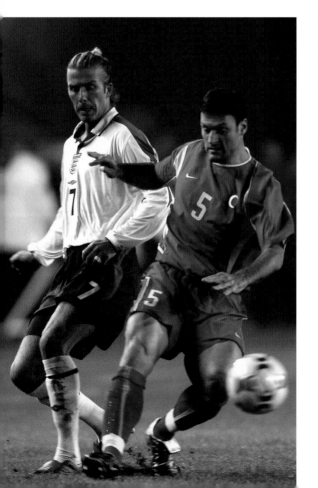

The final qualifiers for the Euro 2004 finals in Portugal climax with a decider in Turkey. The confrontation between Beckham and Alpay provides a secondary focus of the game!

DAVID BECKHAM
Manchester United/Real Madrid
Right midfield
64 international caps (as of October 2003)

A truly exceptional person and a great footballer, David Beckham has become the most talked about player of all time. He lives between the football world and that of a celebrity and copes well with both. As captain of the England team he handles the press conferences as proficiently as he performs on the field and at twenty-eight years old he has the chance to create many records, having over 60 caps already, along with 13 goals. His leadership in difficult matches has proved inspirational to the team, driving them to raise their game in order to get results. His transfer to Real Madrid can only further improve his play and his England contribution.

MICHAEL OWEN
Liverpool
Striker
53 international caps (as of October 2003)

In 1998 Michael Owen made his international debut and in five years already garnered 50 caps. Given freedom from injury he is well on course to beat Peter Shilton's record 125 appearances: couple that with a current tally of 24 goals and he could also surpass Bobby Charlton's existing record of 49. Whilst he may be on the small side, he copes remarkable well. Owen is fast and has a powerful shot but that is not the full package – his heading ability, reaction speed and quick thinking also play a major part in his amazing success.

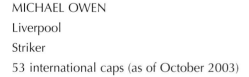

INDEX

INDEX

If you are interested in purchasing other books published by Tempus,
or in case you have difficulty finding any Tempus books
in your local bookshop, you can also place orders directly through our website

www.tempus-publishing.com

or from

BOOKPOST
Freepost, PO Box 29,
Douglas, Isle of Man
IM99 1BQ
Tel 01624 836000
email bookshop@enterprise.net